D0353913

LIS - LIBRARY

Date
21/1/...e-Riv

Order
...569103

University of Chester

WITHDRAWN

# CLASSROOM
## IN THE
# CLOUD

## SEIZING THE ADVANTAGE IN THE BLENDED LEARNING REVOLUTION

ALEX MCGRATH

**First Published 2014**

by John Catt Educational Ltd,
12 Deben Mill Business Centre, Old Maltings Approach,
Melton, Woodbridge IP12 1BL
Tel: +44 (0) 1394 389850 Fax: +44 (0) 1394 386893
Email: enquiries@johncatt.com
Website: www.johncatt.com

© 2014 Alex McGrath
All rights reserved.

No part of this publication may be reproduced,
stored in a retrieval system, transmitted in any form or by any means,
electronic, mechanical, photocopying, recording, or otherwise,
without the prior permission of the publishers.

Opinions expressed in this publication are those of the contributors
and are not necessarily those of the publishers or the editors.
We cannot accept responsibility for any errors or omissions.

ISBN: 978 1 909717 19 0

Set and designed by Theoria Design Limited
www.theoriadesign.com

Printed and bound in Great Britain
by Cambrian Printers, Aberystwyth.

*For Mum and Dad*

# CONTENTS

...to abandon completely ... the opinion that the sun stands still at the centre of the world and the earth moves, and henceforth not to hold, teach, or defend it in any way whatever, either orally or in writing.
**The Inquisition's injunction against Galileo, 1616**

There is nothing more difficult to take in hand, more perilous to conduct, or more uncertain in its success, than to take the lead in the introduction of a new order of things.
**Niccolo Machiavelli, *The Prince* (written 1513, published 1532)**

*Sapere Aude! (Dare to be Wise!)*
**Motto of my alma mater, The Manchester Grammar School, founded by Hugh Oldham, Bishop of Exeter, 1515**

# Preface

## by Mungo Dunnett, founder/owner of Mungo Dunnett Associates

T HERE IS a simple truth about education: people care about it. That is why it attracts such attention, whether well-intentioned and well-informed (or not), from parents, politicians and peddlers of educational snake oil. But at the heart of it – sheltering as best it can from the business models, the metrics, the cost efficiencies – remains the fundamental bond, between the teacher and the pupil. Where it works (and we have all seen it work) it inspires a search for knowledge, for debate, for *engagement*. And yet it remains maddeningly difficult to produce, in spite of the fortunes spent by both maintained and independent sectors in recent times. The search for answers – affordable answers, both for educationalists and families – goes on.

The strangeness, in fact, is that UK schooling, whilst under continuing intense scrutiny, has been so slow to explore the development of blended learning beyond our shores. It offers pragmatic (and badly needed) answers to schools' economic and pedagogical issues, not only in terms of cost efficiency but also in terms of that precious teacher-pupil bond, and in better outcomes for the child. And that is what I like about this book. It avoids the wearying default to educational faddishness, and is couched stubbornly in terms of adoption: recognising and avoiding the pathology of school resistance to innovation; and retaining the centrality of teachers, though in a newly defined role.

This is a sobering account of UK schools' travails, and few can argue that our sector requires substantial adjustment to teaching methods which appear either financially or educationally unsustainable. Technology brings with it its own fears and misapprehensions; but business, and our children's childhoods, have been transformed by technology. The gift of this book is to show that technology – carefully, sensitively adopted – can address our sector's seemingly intractable issues; and in so doing, to deliver what is right for each child. This will not be easy – and it may be that not all the answers are yet here – but if we care, we owe it to ourselves to look hard.

# Introduction

## We can't duck the issue

**No other institution faces challenges as radical as those which will transform the school.**
Peter Drucker, Post Capitalist Society, 1993

When was the last time you looked at a duck?

I mean *really looked?*

I once heard a colleague talking about ducks, and popped out at lunchtime to the local university campus. There is a lovely large lake there, and it is populated by all manner of waterfowl, but it was the mallard which was my particular quarry on this fateful January morning in 2011.

Turn the page and take a look. Notice anything?

Perhaps not. And I don't think that I would have done either had it not been for the fact that my colleague had pointed it out earlier. However, what he had said about ducks had been so revolutionary that I was unable from that point on ever to look at the creatures in the same way again. Take a really close look at the duck's face, and you will see that in fact ducks are trying (rather unsuccessfully) to disguise themselves by wearing little dog masks.

Do you see it? Take a look at this one.....

In fact, ducks worldwide are all attempting to dress up as small, happy yellow dogs....

From that day onwards I have never been able to look at a duck without a chuckle as I focus slightly differently and take in the little yellow dog mask. My whole way of looking at ducks has shifted, and the shift cannot be corrected. Such shifts come along once in a while. We have something familiar, and which we were brought up with. We never question it, and take it for granted. Then suddenly something transforms our view entirely. We focus on a new aspect, and see new relevance.

Thomas Kuhn, in his book *The Structure Of Scientific Revolutions* (1962), called this a paradigm shift. His work challenged the theory that scientific advancement was an evolving process by suggesting that in fact all scientific progress was 'a series of peaceful interludes ... punctuated by intellectually violent revolutions in which one conceptual world view is replaced by another'.

Headier stuff than ducks, perhaps, but you get the picture? Ideas create perceptions, and we are never able to view the world in the same way ever again. Our intellectual understanding has been hijacked by the new concept. Recently this has happened in education. This book will examine the implications of a paradigm shift in our view of good learning, good teaching, and indeed the very notion of school. At the end of this book, I hope that none of you will look at education in the same way again. As with ducks, you will see through aspects of the new disguise and still know what real education is. However, you might have amended your view of what it might look like.

Now that we know about the dog masks we just have to accept that ducks look a little funnier than they used to, and get used to the new perspective.

There is not a lot that we can do about it. In the same way, we could decide that if a change in our perception of education has come about it will remain. We should get on with it. But there is an important difference, of course.

Ducks always looked like this. We just did not notice the detail until it was pointed out to us. However, education is changing radically and fundamentally. While the revolution in our perception of the duck's face is purely one of idea and perspective, the technological revolution in teaching and learning is something genuinely new. As a result, it is potentially disruptive. As an individual reader you may be excited by this disruption or terrified by it. What is clear is that you will need to confront it, because while your view of what good education is may well remain the same, your view of teaching and learning will become radically altered, if it has not been already. There may be some of you who never even noticed that it was here, and like your new perspective on a duck's face will only see the difference because of reading this book. I hope that you will be glad that you did.

In my previous book, *Lifting Our Heads* (2013), I put forward the argument that the independent education sector in the UK was facing a number of challenges. These centred mainly about the fact that our schools were becoming less affordable for those who may wish their children to attend them. I did not set out to be a harbinger of doom, however. I made the case that independent schools were centres of excellence, powerfully led, and exceptional value for money. The job at hand was to demonstrate the fact while addressing the affordability of such schools and the political challenge which that created for them.

Similarly *Classroom In The Cloud* is not a book by a Luddite complaining that something nasty from across the Atlantic threatens the education of our children, the jobs of our teachers, and our very existence as schools. There are some who would make such accusations. I am not one of them. This book is a celebration of our schools, and what I am convinced they are capable of. It is also an encouragement to school leaders to embrace the opportunity which online and blended learning presents for us. But we must acknowledge that it will take a lot of hard work and careful planning, which UK schools should ideally attempt together, to ensure that the disruptive forces are harnessed by us as opportunities rather than overwhelming and destroying us. This will require independence of thinking, independence of leadership, and yet co-operation across independent and state sectors. Government initiatives and centralised control, or 'one size fits all' models will spell disaster, and hamstring us in our ability to adapt effectively.

BYOD (Bring Your Own Device) is with us already, but it is concerning how many schools are taking the plunge without too much understanding of the wider issues involved. BYOD requires a strategy. There are enormous ramifications to creating the capability in schools to learn on the move. Across the Atlantic, online and blended learning in the USA in both Higher

Education and K-12 schools is becoming a destabilising and political issue. We know that British politicians take enormous interest in the educational initiatives of other countries. Free schools had their roots in charter schools in the States, as well as the Swedish free school movement. Undoubtedly there will be someone in Whitehall at this moment scrutinising the pros and cons of virtual schools and blended learning in the US, and as the financial savings may be substantial it stands to reason that the Department of Education will soon be trumpeting the benefits of e-learning within the UK maintained sector. Pilots are running right now!

So, the purpose of this book is to focus the minds of teachers and leaders within UK schools on a task at hand: to face the potential disruptive forces of the online education revolution calmly, nimbly and with confidence. I believe that we can do so, but our response requires planning and co-ordination. It cannot be haphazard, and nor, probably, can we take on the threat as individual schools. This is something which requires cross-association collaboration if we are to address related underlying issues such as affordability, teacher performance, teacher pay, and the maintenance of the quality education we offer – not to mention the confidence of leading the field in e-learning as we do in other aspects of educational provision. This book aims to help UK schools to remain ahead of the game – whether they are independent fee-paying establishments, or the centres of excellence within the maintained sector. I whole-heartedly believe that blended learning in particular presents an opportunity for strengthening and promoting the quality offering our schools represent in comparison to alternative providers.

We begin by considering the obstacles to change which we all face as incumbents in a Victorian system which is no longer fit for purpose. Thereafter we will consider the major sticking point: how to train and prepare our teachers for what is coming, ensuring that they embrace the change rather than become Luddites, for the benefit of our schools and our pupils.

The subsequent chapters define the terminology while assessing what is actually going on out there in the wider world, and its implications for UK schools. We critically examine the future of learning and teaching, and consider how our schools might need to adapt in the face of the challenges presented, and to take a part in creating the future so that we can ride the wave rather than become engulfed, and drown. We assess the benefits to children and education professionals of the new ways of learning, and then outline practical strategies to dealing with disruption and planning for it rather than becoming suddenly swamped; having to tread water and take drastic action after the event. We also consider how Cloud computing may help or hinder us.

The final chapters will then focus the lens specifically upon the independent leadership of schools in the UK, and how we are uniquely placed to capitalise on the changes and acquire a competitive advantage because of our market position; our independence; and the quality which we already have; both at home and internationally. This section in particular should engender hope and confidence in the light of the challenges before us.

I am tremendously excited about the potential for meaningful change within education which the technological revolution presents to us. I am firmly of the belief that children and teachers will be the beneficiaries, and learning will become more meaningful for all. The problem is not the revolution but, as with all revolutions, the counter-revolutionary intransigence which will seek to strangle the revolution at birth. If we do not engage with the issues purposefully and honestly, this reactionary mind set will grow among our governing bodies, senior leadership, teachers, and the parents of our pupils. Those who are in positions of primacy at the time of revolutions are always those most in danger, and with most to lose. Our children, however, do not share our pre-conceived ideas and suspicions. They are growing up in an online world. They are inquisitive, excited and excitable. They will carry this revolution, because to them it is not revolutionary. They are engaged with it, and it makes sense. We must face it. We cannot duck the issue!

# Chapter 1

# The Incumbent's Dilemma – why many of us cannot change

**There is no human change without emotion and there is
no human emotion that does not embody a momentary or
momentous process of change.**

Andy Hargreaves (2004)

When we consider the future, the majority of us consider ways in which
we can achieve success. We do not begin by envisaging the demise of our
schools as inevitable, and certainly not as a fate which lurks around the next
corner. And yet we live in a world in which there are very few certainties.
As long ago as 1993, the 'virtual organisation' was being envisaged:

> …a virtual company is a new organisational model that uses
> technology to dynamically link people, assets and ideas.
> (*Business Week*, Feb 8, 1993).

Technological innovation has caused disruption to the way we shop, the way
we watch films, and the way we take pictures. It has changed the way we
interact with our friends and families. It opens extraordinary possibilities
while demolishing the bastions of familiarity with which we grew up. In the

Middle East, dictatorships which stood for decades have been brought down – not by leftist radicals or right-wing religious fanatics, but by ordinary, leaderless people united by a common cause and a means to communicate. There is a breathtaking arrogance in the assumption that the great British school will endure such a storm. To fail to engage with this issue will have devastating consequences, not least in the human cost likely of such changes. Teachers will lose their jobs. Communities may lose their schools. Mistakes will be made, and there will be casualties as a result of such mistakes. Children themselves will have their education disrupted while various well-meaning, but misguided experiments occur. I am a parent of three children between the ages of nine and fourteen. This matters to me! I am the Head of a school which is seeking to keep ahead of the game in a competitive environment with a discerning group of parents who seek reassurance that we steward their children correctly and, while engaging them in the business of learning, prepare them pragmatically for the world beyond school. This matters to them, and to the very future of my school.

In his book, *The Search For Survival: Lessons from Disruptive Technologies* (2012), Henry C. Lucas Jr. considers the mistakes of previous major players in business who had to face technological change. For many of these, the very fact that they were the market leaders – massive names like Kodak, Blockbuster and Borders (the US *Waterstones* equivalent) – was instrumental in their downfall. They suffered from the 'Incumbent's Dilemma'. This is briefly explained as follows:

   a. The Incumbent, (a market leader), is master of all it surveys.
      A household name, with a brand so secure that it barely need advertise, such is the subliminal nature of its reach into consumer consciousness.
   b. Along comes an innovator with a new piece of technology,
      delivering innovation either of products, services or business model.
   c. The incumbent faces a dilemma! It can:
         a. Morph its own business model to accommodate competition and new opportunities
         b. Abandon its existing business model and adopt a new one
         c. Fail, resulting in merger, buyout or liquidation.

The first two options are both possible *if* the incumbent recognises the threat or opportunity within the new technology. In the first instance this threat must be matched, and the opportunity realised in order for the incumbent to keep doing what it has been doing as far as possible. For instance, had Blockbuster immediately recognised the threat from Netflix and begun a DVD by mail programme in time, they would have enhanced their own competence to serve their customers while neutralising the impact of Netflix's new way of doing business.

In the second scenario, the incumbent takes the radical and brave decision that the technology is so disruptive to the way things have been done before that the incumbent itself must go with this change, radically altering course. Change is difficult in any organisation, and this type of change is particularly hard – even traumatic – as it requires the acknowledgement of the entire organisation that life will never be the same again, and so agreeing that change is absolutely necessary. This requires extremely keen foresight, a willingness to reflect, a full understanding of the nature of the coming disruption, and the excellent communication within the organisation to pull off the change. It also requires the sheer guts to leap, uncertain that customers will leap with you. In short, it is well-nigh impossible for a successful business to achieve. Most companies willing to shift so radically are already suffering, and change comes more through desperation than foresight. They are looking failure in the face, and so know beyond doubt that change must happen.

Many incumbents do not adapt in either of these ways. They fail. In a business context they find themselves having to merge with someone more successful; are bought for their assets and customers, facing inevitable change as new owners look to make radical adaptation; or are liquidated completely as washed up companies unable to realise value or competitiveness in the market place any longer. This occurs when the leaders in an organisation say that the new kid on the block is actually not a threat, and so they do not take steps to deal with him. Instead of dismissing threats, leaders should attempt to name the likely impact of new technologies on their business, or encourage their own people to investigate and suggest the impact. But successful companies will see no reason to change a successful model. They do not change until the disruption has occurred all around them. Then the collapse is swift and devastating.

Google are in the innovation and technology business. They do not look at new technology and ignore it. They acquire it. They are then able to turn the innovation into something they might use, or can discard it without a competitor damaging them.

The best UK schools are the envy of the world. Our teachers and school leaders have degrees from top universities, are well trained both prior to commencing their contracts as teachers, and then on the job thereafter. They are regularly inspected, and have time invested in their professional development. School leaders are similarly bright and talented. Governing bodies bring insights of industry, law, local government, construction, and a myriad of other sectors to our school leadership. We have excellent leadership, excellent staff, excellent facilities, and a long and proud history of educating young people. We have even exported our education systems and examinations around the world. British schools and school systems have been sponsored or enfranchised by famous independent schools such as Wellington College, Repton, Haileybury or Dulwich. Private venture capitalists have built groups of schools which deliver the UK curriculum, such as Nord Anglia (whose schools are now located in North America, Eastern and Central Europe, the Middle East and Far East Asia). Cambridge International Examinations are taken by students in every conceivable corner of the globe. Partly this is because English is the *lingua franca* which opens doors to success. Partly it is because our educational traditions and expertise are desirable and respected. Sitting proudly above all this are the names of our famous educational institutions: Oxford and Cambridge; Eton and Harrow. Education UK is to all intents and purposes a brand as powerful as Nike, Disney, Amazon, or Ford. But our greatest educational establishments have something which even the heavyweight brands of international business can only dream of: a durability which has lasted for centuries. My own school, King's Ely in Cambridgeshire, has more than 1300 years of continuous education at its heart. A monastic community founded in the 7th century required musicians for the cathedral church, and educated the choir. Our choristers are still part of the cathedral foundation community, and take a full and active part in the life of our school with almost a thousand other students. We worship in the cathedral as a school – one of the greatest cathedrals in the world. We work and live in buildings around the cathedral close which span every century since the Norman Conquest. We are a school which attracts students of more than twenty nationalities, as well as serving a wide geographical location within the East of England around Cambridge. We can be confident in our curriculum and our wide-ranging co-curricular programme of sports, outdoor education, drama, the Arts, lectures, debating and, of course, music. We are a successful, enduring, fine school. We can be very confident in what we do. The passage of time has allowed the school to adapt to changes as dramatic as the Reformation and the English Civil War. We would not have remained as a successful school without the ability to adapt and be flexible, or indeed to take on new challenges and re-invent ourselves. Even when the monastic community was dissolved by Henry VIII, our school survived as The King's School, Ely. Schools like ours are the ultimate 'incumbents': leaders in their field – in our case the provision of education.

This makes sense, so why would an incumbent fail to adapt? What possible reason could these highly successful businesses have for making such a disastrous call, staffed as they are with talented, experienced people, and with a history of success? Well there are eight reasons, in actual fact, which might cause a successful leading incumbent in an industry to contribute to its own failure to perceive the disruption that it is facing, and to which it must respond:

1. Denial
2. History
3. Resistance to change
4. Mindset
5. Brand
6. Sunk costs
7. Profitability
8. Lack of imagination

Let us take these various factors in turn:

## Denial

Education involves a pupil and a teacher. There are various tools which the teacher can employ in order to stimulate the pupil, but the teacher is always necessary. This has been the case throughout history. The very idea that a machine, and the pupil's interaction with the machine, may threaten the existence of the teacher/pupil relationship is anathema to most educators, parents, and indeed the children themselves. Nevertheless, the precedent now exists for an online school, virtual learning, and even complete independence from a teacher. The belief in the primacy of the teacher is the source of denial. In 1997, a UK government recruitment campaign aimed at teachers carried the line '*Nobody forgets a good teacher*'. The flipside, of course, is that many people have also experienced poor teachers. In addition, there has been an enormous emphasis lately on the importance of developing pupils who are independent learners. The didactic approach to pedagogy is becoming seen to be old hat. Even in the Far East – those countries which top the PISA league tables for mathematics and sciences: China and South Korea – the didactic approach is being reappraised by government leaders and educationalists who are concerned that in the knowledge economy and the instant gratification of curiosity provided by search engines, the need for creativity, critical thinking, discernment and collaboration are more important skills than the ability to regurgitate facts. A teacher as the 'guide on the side', rather than the 'sage on the stage' is gaining enormous currency – and rightly so. However, this is indicative of the changes which are happening in education, and in the world at large. In the age of the search engine, knowledge is readily available. The job of the teacher is no longer to impart knowledge for a student to hold in its head. Indeed, teachers need not know anything at all. The most successful teachers are now those who can demonstrate that they can engage, stimulate and encourage their students to find out for themselves. They are facilitators of learning, and not fountains of knowledge. The next step, naturally, is to develop a learner who no longer needs such a guide. Developing such a learner as quickly as possible is important. We are teaching children discernment, not facts. We are allowing them to develop the skills to learn independently of anyone. Teachers are arguably digging their own graves. In a later chapter I ask the question whether teachers are turkeys who are voting for Christmas.

In the very best schools – those judged outstanding by Ofsted, or the leading establishments within the independent sector in particular – denial is a critical factor. As I mention above, many of our best grammar and private schools have been in existence for centuries. Names such as Eton, Harrow and Rugby are synonymous with quality. The HMC is a brand in its own right, with its tag line 'Leading Independent Schools'. The very best schools believe that they are institutions of enduring quality. They do what they do very well. They are naturally very good at evolving and adapting. Any novel technology will be the latest in a long line of innovations which these schools have either dismissed or embraced in the past. There is no need to change the model for such schools. Their self-confidence is borne from a long period at the top of the tree. Unless leaders of these schools, and those who aspire to be like them, are willing to ask that question of themselves: 'Are we becoming out of date?' or unless the technology offers opportunities for a much more efficient model of schooling which renders the old way untenable, such schools will fail to understand the innovation, and will not invest time in deciding how to best respond. It is easier to deny that the technology will disrupt than to figure out what the impact on the business will be. Related to denial is the next factor...

## History

This is a main cause of leading businesses failing to act in the face of disruption. It is naturally linked to the reasons for denial. As Lucas points out, Kodak had enjoyed thriving business for over a hundred years and had become one of the most recognised brands on Earth. Why would any of its employees have predicted a collapse as spectacular as that which befell the firm? Our schools have been here for far longer. My own can claim origins of well over a thousand years. Schools exist on reputation. Most schools are local. Some of the greatest schools are international in their reputations. Schools acquire reputations because of previous success in examination results, in teaching, or in turning out well-rounded students. In many regions, parents attended the school, as did their parents before them. They carry the reputation of an establishment from when they were children into the next generation. Without radical changes, schools retain their reputations – and especially those which are particularly strong academically. Success breeds success. A successful history can breed something else as well: arrogance, complacency, and denial. And in fact, many parents are more transient these days, and no longer place their children in the school which they themselves attended. They have less personal history with the school. They are more discerning as a consequence, judging the school on what it provides now, and how it will provide for their children's future. With no emotional or historical attachment of their own, parents are less forgiving and more demanding. This is not necessarily a bad thing. It can serve to keep a school on its toes, and ensure that a school is more 'customer-focused', to use business parlance. But this erodes the historical clout of a school...especially a school whose history is contributing to its denial.

Now I am well aware that the latter sentence will cause uproar. "Not my school", you may be saying. "We are always looking to stay ahead of the game, developing initiatives, investing in facilities and, yes, in technology. We are not arrogant. We know that it is competitive out there. The inspections keep us on our toes, too".

I understand. I agree. The best schools are very good at research, reflection, innovation in practice, sharing, networking, investment, and developing excellence. They know what they do, and how to continue to do it well. They are focused on achieving what they have been achieving for decades – and even centuries. But History deceives us that all is a smooth path to progress. Remember the quotation from Kuhn about a series of peaceful interludes punctuated by violent revolutions in which one conceptual world view is replaced by another.

I am an historian. History can be about facts, but it is also very much about interpretations of those who record it. It is about both substance and spin. History can give us a broad sweep in which trends and gradual evolution may be observed. It also gives us key moments, tipping points, sparks to ignite fires. The micro-history of the past few years in education is important to scrutinise rather than the macro when we consider the real and potential impact of technological innovations on schools, and how schools can adapt, or are adapting. We will be doing just that in Chapter 3. The point is that the events and flashpoints of history do not necessarily reveal the full extent of their importance at the time they occur. At the outbreak of World War One, a major conflagration was accepted. People understood that many thousands would perish. They did not necessarily see the multi-million body count, the end of Empire, emancipation of Women, the rise of Nazism and the death of Innocence.

Unless our schools are alive to the flashes and rumbles of today, they will not think through the ramifications for tomorrow. Schools are extraordinarily conservative institutions. Past success is no guarantee of future success. The internet age has changed the landscape. It has changed the attitude of the world to knowledge. It has brought forth the need for creativity, discernment and learning habits to be paramount in education. School curricula and structures of staffing, facilities and resources are yet to catch up. Changing wholesale the way we teach, learn and organise ourselves as schools is an extraordinarily demanding task. This brings us to the third factor of the incumbent's dilemma:

## Resistance to change

Ken Robinson's famous TED talk in Monterey, California in February 2006 is the most watched of all time. In it he argued that 'Schools Kill Creativity'. As I write in June 2014 there have been 26,846,620 people who have watched this talk. Eight Years. All those people. No doubt many of these have shared his ideas widely. No doubt, in view of the subject matter, an enormous number of this online audience have been educators who have spread the word within their schools. And yet, what has changed? This is one of the most influential 18-minute speeches ever given. It has heavily influenced the thinking of many educational leaders. But the system he decried, in many ways, remains exactly the same almost a decade later.

Arguably the problem is that human nature is resistant to change. Undoubtedly, many of Ken Robinson's critics regard him as an idealist. It is not practical to simply tear up the blueprint for our schools and start again. Children are still learning. They are learning the things which allow them to demonstrate achievement in examinations. They are learning the things which colleges and businesses want to judge their entry level students and employees on (although this may be contested, because in an interview questions will focus on experience, adaptability, creativity, resilience and flexibility). Parents understand the old way of doing things and, in the West, our education system has helped us to achieve economic supremacy and a certain amount of political freedom. We are very comfortable, thank you ... and it all seems like such an effort! "If it ain't broke, don't fix it", we may say. Robinson says that it is broke, actually. We should look at it, and see where it needs mending. Can an entire education system really scrutinise itself when we believe that it takes a lot for a large company, a small shop, a family, or even an individual person to take that step outside and reflect? To do so while remaining divorced from the emotional attachment to that which you have been involved with, brought up with or, for those in charge, have created is enormously difficult. And yet, disruption requires that we do just that. The next factor stems from being within a system...

## Mindset

If someone is within a system or a business which is pretty clear in what it does, or sells, they will naturally acquire a mindset that conforms. If the employees of a school have a particular view of what a 'good' education is, they will have difficulty in regarding a different educational model as being good if what they value from their own model is eradicated or at least threatened by the new one. The mindset concerning education being best delivered by a subject specialist within a classroom to 20 or 30 children conspires to feed denial that a model removing the teacher, or delivering to 10,000 students online, may be better for the school, the teacher, or the children. This works to hinder a response to the innovator – either a response which positively embraces the innovation, or in deciding one which best deals with it so that it is eradicated from the system. With a fixed mindset, there simply is no response. But if an innovation is neither challenged, nor embraced and subsumed within the current system it is free to evolve and disrupt those with a denial mindset. This is when the technological innovation becomes disruptive: maybe not at first, but down the line. And when it grows and develops in strength and disruptive power it can be truly devastating. Schools have usually been pretty good at embracing technology. First came a TV in the classroom to demonstrate videos. The Amazon Rainforest was suddenly available as a visual representation in a geography classroom in Hull. The ability to inspire a child through the visual apprehension of the moving image was caught on to by teachers. At best, a video clip of a minute or two was engaging and illustrative. It still required the teacher to adapt the clip, and to deliver it within his teaching. However, the worst of the technology was also present. It allowed the lazy teacher to no longer need to teach. The video stood in for the teacher who was ill or on a course. The video spoke for itself, and the teacher stood back from the hard work of explaining and innovating, and merely flicked a switch to become babysitter, or to get on with marking while the class goggled at a 30-minute film, and were made to take notes to help with a written exercise which might absorb them in the final 30 minutes of the lesson.

The result of this was a lack of teaching, and a lack of engagement between teacher and pupil. But information was imparted to those with the listening or note-taking skills. The teacher had removed himself successfully from the education process. Video, however, was insufficient. Good teachers realised how it could be a tool used well, or a poor substitute for the inspiring educator. Video was replaced by the interactive whiteboard, and the video clip became part of a PowerPoint slide of the teacher who was willing to learn how to incorporate it into a multi-media presentation. Schools have spent hundreds of thousands – even millions of pounds – on providing their staff with interactive whiteboards, PCs, laptops and whole classrooms full of equipment to help teachers to deliver teaching in a classroom to students with a whole host of expensive tools and toys. Often, these technological innovations do not disrupt the teaching mindset. They are just other tools which allow the former methodology to persist, with slightly different presentational panache. 'Death by PowerPoint' is a phenomenon in schools and training departments of every business in the world which has a computer, a screen, a deliverer of information and an audience of learners. The education mindset of show and tell has not changed. It is not an innovation. Where such a mindset persists, schools will continue to waste money on resources which sparkle and shine, but in the hands of ham-fisted and unskilled teachers and students are as yawn-making as a poorly-used textbook or chalk and slate. The innovative teacher is the key. The teacher able to use the tools to excite and inspire. The mindset which resists innovation in educational method is the mindset which says that what we need is only good teachers who understand the new tools. But the disruption does not come from new gizmos and kit. This is technological innovation, but not of the disruptive kind. Technology is too often seen in our schools as hardware and software. The disruptive technology is that which calls for a new business model for schools – and that is so hard for us to conceive because we believe we know what a good education is. People used to know how to sell books. We would go to a store, browse and buy. Stores knew that we liked to browse, and so the more innovative ones offered coffee shops, comfy sofas, and reviews of new titles by the expert readers who worked behind the tills and served you your coffee and engaged you in conversations about books. They stocked the shelves and the stockrooms, and it was all very comforting, reassuring and expensive. It still is. I love going to Waterstones. In moments of weakness I succumb to the aroma of Colombian ground coffee, read the intro to a paperback, and walk out with my loyalty card stamped and a sense of well-being. Mostly, though, I buy my books from Amazon. It's easier, cheaper and I love receiving the book in the post. I rip open the cardboard packaging with genuine excitement. It's a different way of doing business, with a different kind of customer experience ... but it is infinitely more successful. This book will argue that while the mindset about education, and the belief in what is good about traditional schools, will survive, it will become harder for this to survive in every town and village. It will become too expensive to deliver. It will become less desirable and convenient for many people. The disruption of blended and online education will threaten traditional teaching methods (except where inspirational teaching is known to exist), and teachers who are not inspirational will not survive. Schools without inspirational teachers will perish as well. There will be other choices available to the discerning parent and student.

## Brand

A great brand is something which all businesses strive for. How could this possibly lead to a loss of competitive advantage where disruptive innovations are concerned? I mentioned before that Education UK, while not an actual brand in its own right, has a brand quality to it. Education in and from the UK carries reassurance, integrity, creativity and history alongside it. In October 2013, I took part in the British Council's attempt to promote our boarding schools in China.

The trade mission, preceded by visits to China by Boris Johnson and George Osborne and showcasing a host of British industries, was bedecked in the red, white and blue of the Union Flag, and the creativity, innovation and inspiration of our education system, alongside focus on the individual student were all wrapped up in the brand, the messaging.

In this example, the brand was important in selling the UK. Education fit into the wider British Council and UK government message. The other brand identity of UK education is the traditional long-lasting brand of Oxford and Cambridge, Eton and Rugby. These reassure. Their longevity is their strength, as well as the quality of their offering. CIE examinations, with their attachment to Cambridge, and textbooks produced by Cambridge University Press, are reassuring qualifications which underline A levels and iGCSEs as gold standard qualifications which can be trusted as an international currency, exchangeable for places in education institutions world-wide. But will this emphasis on tradition and stability fit with an innovative, forward-looking online educational delivery method? In the world of Coursera MOOCs, which will now certificate courses, are traditional bricks and mortar institutions going to seem archaic and fusty? At some point, the reassuring stability may become old-fashioned. Our education system needs to think through ways in which the innovation and inspirational aspects of our brand come to the fore, and decisions need to be made about whether the traditional should lose emphasis or be re-packaged. Meanwhile, this is not only something which our great public schools and universities need to consider. Education is a global export for us, and the market place is a global one as well. Meanwhile, at home the aspects of our schools such as uniform, house systems, management structures, departmental organisation, moral values, and religious affiliations, have their foundation in our educational history, and the traditions such as the administration of our Empire, our examination structures, and Acts of Parliament which shaped our free provision of excellent schools. The political focus which education attracts due to the billions spent from public funds on buildings, facilities, teachers' salaries and pensions make this history important in the crafting of our future. Education of the standard which we believe should proliferate in our country in order to keep us at the top of the world is incredibly expensive. We need to maintain our world position. Our politicians are desperately interested in ensuring that we do so. The Great Britain brand is vital to maintain. All UK education has tradition and stability as roots that ground it, and yet the innovation, creativity and individual opportunity which we seek to promote overseas requires an authenticity which stems from more than Eton and Oxbridge. It needs to be felt pulsing in the heartbeat of our schools today. This creates a fertile ground for innovation and creativity in the education of our children. Schools which lead will be favoured by our politicians. If schools stick to what they know, the politicians will impose what they feel to be necessary to ensure that our schools are on message and fit with the UK brand. Both our maintained and independent sectors need to take note.

## Sunk costs

And it is all so incredibly expensive, this education business! We have invested so much in it that when the Coalition government took over the reins of leadership in 2010 they found that the cupboard was bare. This is on a national level, with implications for the provision of equipment, facilities and teaching in our maintained schools. The independent sector, meanwhile, has invested inordinate sums in a facilities arms race. At first, independent schools would compete with one another to demonstrate their facilities were better than the neighbouring independent school. Since New Labour education initiatives, and enormous public spending on flagship maintained sector schools, Building Schools for the Future; inflation of salaries for leadership; the Academies Programme; The National College for School Leadership; UTCs; Free Schools, and more, the independents need to justify their fees by demonstrating a differentiation of quality which frankly only money can buy.

Education in the UK has therefore sunk an enormous amount into provision. Increasingly, this has included technology. Hardware, software, network systems, staffing and training costs are a considerable chunk of a school's budget. Many of those making decisions about funding know little about the technical implications of what they are spending, and so are reliant on the few with the knowledge and expertise to advise them. Having spent large amounts, it is difficult for a board of governors to swallow hard and invest more because they are faced with the fact that there is another version of the software, or there needs to be a further extension of the network. Sunk costs, an accounting class will say, should be ignored. But it is hard to do so when more funds are needed and one is accountable for the financial position in which a school finds itself – especially in hard times, as have proliferated in recent years, and in which other costs to the school such as energy and catering are rising at an alarming rate. Future savings cannot be guaranteed, and yet a new model for schooling, which might generate savings or produce further income streams for schools, requires significant investment which might be a leap of faith. The knowledge of sunk costs added to the uncertainty of future returns on investment are considerable hindrances to all but the most confident or informed of decision-makers in schools committing to building a brave new world. Illustrations from the corporate world include Blockbuster. Faced by Netflix distributing films via the internet, Blockbuster needed to consider its sunk costs in real estate and inventory. All those stores! Not only would changing the Blockbuster business model to imitate and out-perform the new provision Netflix offered require enormous investment in infrastructure, it would also mean working to put its old business out of business. Sunk costs mean people's livelihoods a lot of the time. Could Blockbuster do this to its own people? In schools, creating blended learning or online education models might be more efficient. A school with half as many teachers could reach 20 times more students. But this could make teachers redundant on a massive scale. Can schools really countenance such a pathway? Disposing of buildings might be easy for a business. Many businesses prune staff as a fairly regular matter of course. Their attitude to these sunk costs is less emotional than attitudes to the employees or the buildings of a school, which may have served a community for generations. Education is a people business. It is an emotional business. Tearing up the business model to start again when so much has been invested in people over long periods of time is difficult, and for many decision-makers, impossible.

## Profits

When we are discussing the impact of disruptive technologies, and the reasons for failing to deal with them by incumbents, we are talking primarily about successful incumbents. Businesses who face failure are often prepared to try all manner of methods to survive, or indeed are happy to admit defeat. What makes a technology disruptive is when it changes the old order. When a technology is revolutionary it has the power to topple even those at the top of the tree: the success stories and leaders in their field. In business, many of these leaders are there because they enjoy the most sales, have the most loyal customers, run efficiently and cleverly, and as a consequence have the highest profits. How do schools fit with this?

Schools which are inspected by Ofsted or ISI, and those which emerge with poor reports full of recommendations are again not those who we are concerned with here. Many schools in special measures are offered changes of leadership, have funds invested, and are willing to seize any lifeline available to them. Those schools, however, which enjoy excellent examination results, and whose children are judged to emerge with sound values could be seen to be our success stories. In the independent sector, and increasingly in the maintained free school sector, those schools which can turn a healthy surplus from fee income, trading activities, or sponsorship to support further investment in their infrastructure or facilities have another form of 'profit' by which they might be judged. There are also schools which are run for profit, owned by shareholders, or by venture capitalists wishing to grow schools and families of schools in order to one day sell the chain for a healthy sum. Schools may not be 'normal' or simple businesses, but they certainly have criteria on which we might judge their success. A successful school might justifiably question why their entire *modus operandi* should change to accommodate a new technology when results, facilities, funds or educational outcomes are very impressive.

It is a hard argument to counter. And some schools, as we have mentioned, have enduring reputations because of the quality of outcomes which they have delivered year-on-year. The question really is how long such schools will be able to sustain such success once the disruptive technologies take hold? If, for instance, the technological innovation makes the business of running a school much cheaper, schools who embrace it may be able to develop their staff, and reward them, much more than a traditional school. This could cause a shift in the best staff to the new school. Similarly, this school could afford better facilities, or could further invest in technological provision.

Independent schools in particular should think very carefully. We are becoming increasingly expensive, and unaffordable, for a large section of the population. There are implications to this. We either will experience falling rolls, with falling fee income, or might see that we cannot attract as many top quality students, and so compromise our standards. Both may lead to lower 'profits', either financially, or in terms of academic and educative outcomes for our students. How long could independent fee-paying schools weather such a storm while maintaining their quality status? What might the differences be between those independents who embrace innovations, and those who stick with the tried, trusted and (traditionally) profitable? Bravery will be the factor here, of course. Part of the leap into the unknown is that it will be leap for traditional customers as well. A school which effectively communicates what it is doing to its parents, pupils and staff will be able to take them along, but the risk will naturally be that such customers do not want a new product. The risk of losing traditional customers needs to be weighed against the opportunity of gaining new ones. I talk about parents as customers in schools with no shame. Whether they are fee-paying parents at an independent, or tax-paying parents in a maintained school, each have a certain amount of choice, and are able to move from one type of school to another. Some have more choice than others because of ability to pay, or lack of local provision. If there are innovations in educational delivery systems, the choice for some may dramatically or fundamentally increase. However, if the changes are not well managed on a systemic level by school leaders and political decision-makers there may be poor planning and the diminishing of choice in some localities. It all comes down to the final element of the innovator's dilemma...

## Lack of imagination

How imaginative are we? How creative are we? During the Great Mission to China that I mentioned earlier, the innovation and creativity of our schools, universities, businesses and indeed our country was trumpeted to all. But how far is this aspiration, and how far is it reality? Can we actually envision the future of our education system embracing new technology? If not, we will be less able to plan, and be reactive rather than proactive. Perhaps we can envision the impact of the technology on our systems, but cannot see how we can adapt our individual schools? This requires leadership which is open-minded, creative and innovative, rather than wedded to traditional structures.

Can we lead the imaginative thinking of our stakeholders: governors, politicians, parents, children, suppliers, and service providers?

## How to avoid the incumbent's dilemma?

It may appear that all the eight reasons for failure to respond effectively to disruptive technology are too much for any industry or organisation to overcome. After all, they depend on the incumbent being a market leader. The incumbent is in position because of its history and success. It is counter-intuitive for the incumbent to throw all the causes of its success to one side and to take the disruptive technology to its bosom.

However, the point made by Hank Lucas is that an organisation is not the thing that acts. People act. Those whose job it is to ensure that the innovation is perceived as a disruption, and thereafter harnessed by an organisation to ensure that it is competence enhancing rather than competence threatening in an organisation are its leaders. Actually, Hank Lucas says that managers perform this function. In many industries this may well be the case. But in schools, the agents of change are often teachers. It is teachers that plan lessons and interact with children in the classroom, theatre and sports field each and every moment of the school day. It is teachers who bring innovation and change into the classroom. It is teachers who impact most directly on the lives of their students. Teachers can lead innovation and respond to it, or teachers can run in fear of innovation and hide from it. I believe that leaders in school exist at all levels of our hierarchical structure, and the agency of teachers is enormously powerful. So as managers and school leaders, we need to use our influence to not only raise awareness of the potential disruption to education which technological innovation is bringing, but also to empower those teachers who can lead their colleagues in embracing it. Teachers who have been schooled, and then trained, and then affirmed in their practice through the now-threatened system which has worked and produced results since ancient times. We need to lead these intelligent, competent and highly-skilled people into an unknown in which their intelligence, competence and skills are challenged and scrutinised. Where the professional will feel like a turkey. We need, in effect, to ask these turkeys to vote for Christmas. This requires us to make and execute some very tough decisions: not only to take a risk on an unproven or untested product or course of action, but also to replace people within the school who refuse to accept the need to change. In this endeavour, it is teachers who I suggest should be our allies in persuading other stakeholders, and particularly the politicians, unions, governors and parents, that a new model is required. The first step in ensuring that our actions will be supported involves the training and development of our teachers.

## Chapter 2

# Teachers: turkeys who won't vote for Christmas

**It follows, as night follows day, that if the goals of education systems change as radically as proposed...then the education workforce – especially the teaching profession – will need to change radically too.**

Michael Barber (2000)

S CHOOLS ARE all about children, of course. Or are they? I would suggest that the majority of Headteachers when asked about the main motivation in schools would agree. Ask those same Heads about their staff, and I believe they would acknowledge that their teachers work tirelessly for the benefit of the children, and require the long holidays to recover from the emotional and physical outpouring of a year of relentless selflessness. Our schools are full of wonderful professionals doing their very best to give children the best start in life, a preparation for the future, a place at university, to make them employable, or to take care of them and offer them a safe place. It all depends on the child, and each teacher's own relationship with that child.

So what if we asked our heads to be frank with us, and to ask them about self-interest in the staff room. Are there shirkers and 'jobsworths'? Are there those who avoid doing duties, or marking books, or who turn on a video rather than plan engaging and inspirational lessons? Are there those who would prefer to have a cup of coffee in the staff room rather than roam the corridors (with their coffee), and engage with the children they meet? Are there staff who shoot off and leave the car park before the very first child has sprinted from the gates? Are there staff who moan about having to come to parents' evenings, are always late to supervise a lunch queue, or point blank refuse to take a lunchtime activity? Are there colleagues who sneer at those who take the extra activity, and accuse them of being careerists? Are there those who delight in not having given a detention in 20 years (because they know that they, too, will lose half their lunch hour supervising it)? How many Heads would recognise all of these staff within their schools, and also add for good measure the teachers who refuse to attend training because "you can't teach an old dog new tricks", or who might say, "My results are strong. Why change?"

Of course, all of these exist in every school, alongside the paragons of vocational teaching. This is because schools are filled with people, and people are not perfect. Some are lazy. Some are tired. Some feel beleaguered or bitter or depressed. Some have family crises which impact on their work. Many are sick of initiatives which they had no part in developing. Many are disheartened and sceptical because they have tried and failed to make a difference over and over again with some children. Teachers, being human, often have flaws or lapses in professionalism. They exist in a high pressure context. They feel misunderstood. They often do not feel that what they are doing has been adequately explained. They seek to be treated as adults, but too often feel that they are treated as children, and are not given the courtesy of consultation on major decisions.

On top of this, there is the new phenomenon of performance-related pay being brought in to the maintained sector, which the independent sector is cautiously looking askance at, as yet unaware of the implications for its own teachers.

The history of political imposition, whether from management within schools, or political decision-making beyond, has also created a highly unionised workforce which has secured very favourable working conditions. The generous pension scheme for teachers is a huge bill for government, which is now in the process of being tinkered with. After the past 20 years or so, the teaching profession in the UK has become defensive and spikey, while at the same time enjoying rare privileges. It is a paradoxical profession.

Heads will often say that their best resource is their teaching staff. It is certainly the most expensive resource, with salaries and on-costs accounting for anything up to 75% of an independent school's fee income. Excellent teachers reassure parents, inspire youngsters, develop the school, and achieve excellent results. Poor teachers are the source of parental complaints, disaffected pupils, school stagnation, and under-achievement. This draws the gaze of politicians, school business managers, governing bodies and

Heads. How does a school achieve the Holy Grail of excellence in teaching and learning across all subjects? What does a school do about the one poor teacher who is bringing down the results and reputation of the subject, and by extension the school itself? As a nation, how do we ensure that teaching standards are of the highest quality?

Certainly there is a compelling case for removing those teachers who cannot connect well with children, replacing them with excellent practitioners who can reach far more pupils through blended learning or online provision, and paying these 'star' teachers a little more while making savings on the salaries of those who do not make the mark. It does not take an enormous amount of imagination to envisage maintained sector learning 'hubs' of online provision in a locality, with some school buildings decommissioned, an open university style of blended course for children, and a range of activity camps and courses for children run by expert coaches affiliated to top quality sports clubs, museums, art galleries, theatres and concert halls. Such a novel way of funding education and educational activity would save money in some areas, re-direct it elsewhere, and could be a fantastic way of developing the broader education of young people. Or it could be a logistical headache, a waste of public money, and see the demoralisation of the teaching profession. Why would any but the most confident of teachers collaborate in such a system? In Chapters 4 and 5 we speculate further on the ways schools may change in the future, and use our imaginations to picture a sustainable and exciting future for UK education. Meanwhile, we have the initial problem of what to do with all our teachers? How might they be affected by the online learning revolution? On thinking about these implications, there are some surprising consequences. It is important to point out here that this is all speculation. That is the joy of horizon-scanning. There is a certain amount of playing the soothsayer involved.

Our individual teacher, faced with technological innovation, has a number of paths open, depending on their position now.

## The new entrant

As a younger teacher, it is likely that our new entrant to the profession is pretty conversant with new technology, and able to use a smart phone or tablet for their own purposes. As a result, the use of devices in the classroom holds no fear for them. There would still need to be a training programme within the school to ensure that the new teacher was not over-reliant on one type of device, and playing safe. After all, technological innovation moves quickly. The blended learning scenario would suit this teacher well. In their initial teacher training they could work to perfect their technique in developing their online resources without the distraction of a full teaching timetable absorbing their day. They would be taught the ability to unlearn approaches as a fundamental point of their training, as it would be important that they lead their students in taking on the potential of new devices. They would doubtless need to learn traditional methods as a standby in case of technological failure. The lack of opportunity to practice such techniques would mean a lack of ability in this type of delivery, and so there are implications for schools and teacher training colleges to devise courses and curricula which ensured a minimum level of traditional methods. While the new young entrant will have the customary energy and enthusiasm to take on new techniques, their ability to do so by observation of well-seasoned colleagues may be compromised unless sufficient training has been invested in colleagues with a more traditional background. This could be useful, as the new entrant may be forced by these circumstances into developing innovative lesson plans which can be utilised by their new school. The flattening of hierarchical structures in schools which the new skills may precipitate is an interesting feature which may lead to reorganisation of management and the reward of fresher practitioners with responsibilities much sooner in their careers. This is likely to persist only in the first establishment phases of blended and online learning. Finally, the new entrant may have fewer employment opportunities, as there would be less need for a large teacher workforce due to the possibility of duplicating online content and courses. If they were successful in getting jobs, new entrants may have less direct access to learners, and thereby have less experience in dealing with the changing demands and growing maturity of young people which daily interaction can develop in a new teacher.

## The part-time working parent

The blended learning and online classroom is an exciting and rewarding place for the teacher who is a working parent, and as a consequence has thus far been part-time. The duplication of content to reach many different classes means that timetables in schools are less restrictive, and as a result, the part-timer could teach as many lessons as a full-time member of staff. The flexibility afforded by a virtual classroom also appeals to the part-time worker. Able to plan and prepare lesson materials at a time which suits will allow the teacher to deliver full courses, which may not have been possible within a traditional school. All this could lead to a part-timer being able to earn extra income, as well as holding down jobs in more than one school if necessary. Schools may decide to reward staff by numbers enrolled or remaining enrolled on online courses, as well as the time spent in class for blended learning groups. This may play into the part-timer's hands, because if their online content is consistently strong, they will gain a following of students. The lack of necessity to be in a place of work physically in order to reach the pupils is a fascinating concept and this could give a new lease of life to some part-timers who otherwise would not have been acknowledged, or would not have had the time and ability to contribute as a full-timer would have.

## The excellent teacher

Teachers who are graded as excellent in the traditional setting may well attain a heightened status in the online world. Their showpiece lessons, recorded online, could legitimately enjoy worldwide acclaim. There is the possibility that such teachers might even sell the content of their home-produced online courses to a number of schools, or demand a high price from prospective employers. This introduces the concept of the online teacher as an artist, and a self-employed agent, not tied down to a particular job, school or location. Such teachers may well develop specialisms not only of subject, but also of types of learner. There could be real flexibility for them in the online world if they are willing to put in the time to creating exceptional content. What may have marked these teachers out, however, in the traditional classroom is their connection with their students, and unless this can translate through an online medium, this is no guarantee of online success. These teachers may work very well in a blended learning scenario, in which students sitting virtual online courses come in periodically to see their tutor for guidance. This may restrict the excellent teacher to being available in one institution, but there would be no reason why they should not have several schools whom they serve, and be itinerant. The main issue for the excellent teacher is their capacity to serve their students equally, and I can envisage a range of tiers of students from those who benefit from a bespoke tutoring service, through to those who can enjoy the online courses without direct connection to the teacher. Meanwhile, there would be tiers inbetween. Such a scenario could become very lucrative for top quality teachers, who can monitor the demand for their services and charge accordingly. Schools with a number of these teachers could take some firm decisions about staffing, and develop a suite of truly inspirational courses, refreshed from time to time. The quality control of such courses would be important, and the professionalism of the teacher creating the online content would serve in many ways as a self-regulatory check. To be the star teacher envisaged above, an excellent teacher would need to work exceptionally hard on content of online lessons and materials. An industry of content developers would doubtless follow these frontline teachers, who may even gain by endorsing online materials from different service providers.

## The ordinary teacher

The teachers who would need most convincing to make this leap into blended and online learning would be those who may consider themselves ordinary. This is the vast majority of good staff, working hard for the benefit of the children in schools throughout Britain every day. There are definite threats to jobs and current practices envisaged in the above scenarios. When these teachers consider an online world, they may see the lack of interaction with students on which they thrive. When considering the production of online content for online or blended courses they no doubt see further work in areas in which they lack the confidence or expertise to excel. Schools which are looking to shed staff might use blended or online models to make such cuts, and the threat to morale of such measures, especially in the run-up to such decisions being taken, would be a major source of anguish to many in the teaching profession. Unions would either become the champions of the beleaguered masses, or would buckle under the pressure of trying to support so many. A new Luddism is possible, although on the other hand, there is unlikely to be such an overnight swinging axe that sufficient momentum would be achieved to carry through wholesale changes. The pessimist sees an exodus of unskilled, hapless teachers from schools which are making efficiencies, without the knowledge of where they might turn. Even those remaining within the profession would have different structures within which they might work, with fewer middle managers required due to the reduction in the workforce as a whole, and a bottleneck for promotion created by the retention of the most talented at the expense of those without sufficient diversity of skills. Tougher performance management and quality control mechanisms would be required by schools to maintain the quality of their educational provision online, and some schools would be likely to close as successful providers of online and blended education swept up students who would no longer need to live in a particular catchment area to attend class. On the plus side, however, the ordinary teacher facing such a future has a choice to make. A positive choice would be to acquire further skills, invigorate one's teaching, and enhance one's career prospects. There is a possibility for teachers who are ordinary in the high tension and time-poor system today to discover a new lease of life teaching blended courses, and interacting less frequently, but more meaningfully, with students. The personal nature of the relationship between online learner and teacher may suit some teachers far better than being the form teacher, and chasing the tails of 30 pupils around. Relationships with parents are likely to change significantly. Some pupils from many miles away may not have parents able to interact with the individual teacher, and where problems arise, it is likelier that the school would be dealt with directly. Not all the ramifications for teachers are bad ones. In blended learning institutions, the interactions with pupils will be more focused and specific to work done online. These interactions are likely to be more like seminars and tutorials, with an emphasis on individual progression. The caring teacher will benefit far more from this environment than a crowd control scenario. Also, for those schools whose pupils include those with illness, or with sports commitments which preclude them from taking part in formal schooling, these students will provide new and interesting challenges to teachers teaching them for the first time.

The above scenarios may appear to be fantasy, but in the USA, there are already a large number of blended learning and wholly online schools. Clayton Christensen, in his book *Disrupting Class* (2000), predicted that by

2019 50% of all high school courses in the USA will be delivered online. Politicians have backed this movement:

> The factory model of education is wrong for the 21st Century. Today our schools must prepare all students for college and careers – and do far more to personalize instruction and employ the use of smart technology.
> (US secretary of State for Education, Arne Duncan, 2011 speech).

The interesting thing is that blended learning models in the US school system are out-performing traditional schools in terms of raw results, as the following examples demonstrate:

1. High Tech High School, San Diego, California (4378 students have now graduated): Classes are divided 50:50 with half receiving face-to-face instruction and half an online course. Languages are taught wholly online using Rosetta Stone. 100% of graduates from the K-12 school obtained places at college, and 93% passed the High School Exit Examination at the first attempt, as opposed to a state-wide average of 80%.
2. Rocketship Education, San Jose, California (1328 enrolled): 25% of instruction is online. 93% proficiency in Mathematics and 75% proficiency in language arts, out-performing the state average by 29% and 17% respectively.
3. Florida Virtual School, Orlando, Florida (7000 enrolled): By 2011, this wholly online laboratory at which students met on campus, but had no teacher interface demonstrated results and completion rates which were the same as those in other schools who benefited from face-to-face instruction. The Virtual School pupils benefited from online tutors and supervisors who checked their deadlines and offered email advice. The school had been set up to counter education cuts in the state of California which hit staffing levels.
4. Michigan Virtual School (15,000 enrolled ages 12-18): In 2011 the course completion rate was 84%. The school allows children unable to access certain courses at their often remote and understaffed traditional schools to take additional subjects online and supplement their high school portfolios.
5. Albuquerque Public Schools eCademy, New Mexico (1500 enrolled): 25% the size of other schools in the area, but able to accommodate the same number of students. It achieved a 70% retention rate, compared to a 50% retention rate which it had before moving to a blended learning model.
   (Source: Knewton Blended Learning Infographic on www. knewton.com/blendedlearning)

With such examples creating upturns in various measures of retention, engagement and achievement of students in American schools, not to mention the reduction in costs possible by employing fewer teachers and better utilisation of school buildings, it is hard to believe that UK politicians will not be taking notice. Many of these examples are blended learning scenarios, which continue to be hosted in bricks and mortar schools, engaging classroom face-to-face teachers for some of the courses. They do not spell the end of the teacher, but certainly flip the classroom emphasis from one of teacher direction and knowledge-giving to a model of pupil curiosity and research, followed by teacher reinforcement and intervention. It is this surgical intervention of the teacher in a personalised programme for each child which is believed produces the impressive results.

If the teachers themselves will not vote for Christmas, it is surely not long before politicians announce that Christmas has come. It behoves teachers to get busy and be ready. As school leaders, we should do our level best to empower them, and to help them embrace the changes and ride the wave rather than lose stability and drown in innovation. There is an enormous amount going on out there in the K-12 world. We cannot ignore it.

"Well, good luck, Headmaster. But I can't wait that long. It's not your fault. You've only been in post for two weeks. But that worries me. You're not likely to turn things around quickly enough for my son. By the time there is any significant change he will already be well into his GCSEs. I'm afraid I'm here to tell you that we're withdrawing him at half-term. He'll be starting at the new academy – and I don't expect to pay fees in lieu of notice!"

This final sentence is delivered with a steely air of finality which makes it clear this is not a situation which will be up for negotiation.

# Chapter 3

# What's going on out there, and is it disruption?

**The East Asian economies are witnessing an exponential growth in their investment in education, with the skill in their labour forces already matching that of Australia in Hong Kong, Singapore, Taiwan, Thailand, Malaysia, and other tiger economies ... if we fail to nurture the development of excellence in our young people we will lose out in the global stakes**

B. Lepani, University of Sydney, Australia, 1994

WE HAVE spoken a great deal about disruption, and about technology, without really examining what this means for education as a whole, or education in the UK specifically. In this chapter, we will look at exactly what we mean when we discuss disruptive technology in our context.

To set a background for why now is the time to discuss disruption in UK education we first need to examine two further factors: the recent history of education in the UK, for which I'll focus on the period since 1997, and also the wider context of how technology and other political and economic factors have been affecting education overseas. These two are important to examine because while most of our schools will operate in a pretty specific local context, UK education as a whole takes its place on a global stage, and the global context affects the smallest British rural primary school because of the political interest taken by successive governments in academic standards and outcomes. Meanwhile, the UK independent sector really does operate in a global market place due to the enormous numbers of overseas students who choose to study for part of their education in the UK, while also being courted by schools in other parts of the world: most notably the USA, Canada, Australia, and the Middle East. The growing number of UK curriculum schools becoming available for these children in their home countries is another factor in the equation. An examination of some case studies of how advancement of technology is affecting classroom practice worldwide will then follow before we appraise what 'good learning' is in the online context in Chapter 4.

It will not escape your notice that the quotation which begins this chapter was from a paper produced 20 years ago! The crisis which Australia foresaw at that time led to a 'Declaration of Educational Goals' by the Australian business sector. At that time the issue was economic development and educational investment by the governments of the Asian economies. Now technology brings the possibilities of online learning to a global audience.

So, what do we mean by technology in the context of education? Different businesses use different types of technology in order to provide better value goods and services to their customers. This means that different technologies suit different businesses, and if we are not careful we will not think about our schools and technology in an appropriate way. Often, in schools, we think of technology as 'kit': toys with which we can try and produce whizzier lessons for children in order to somehow excite them. This is certainly part of what we mean by technology, and different pieces of kit with different capabilities and applications help our teachers and learners to do all manner of things differently. One of the biggest single challenges which a school faces is how to keep up with the constantly changing landscape. Once a teacher has mastered one piece of kit, a more advanced version appears, and the finance required for acquisition of further pieces of kit, and for the further training of staff, becomes exponential.

But I think that this is in many ways a rather simplistic view of technology in education. It also comes with a simple choice: a school can invest in it, or can decide that it cannot afford the new kit. Fundamentally, can the new piece of equipment guarantee that the child's learning will be of better quality? What is the real question we are answering when we decide to purchase new equipment? Is it one about learning, outcomes, or keeping up with, or ahead of, the school round the corner? If a new piece of equipment does not fundamentally change what we do, it is not a disruptive technology. It is a nice to have item that may enhance the experience of learning, but there will be other ways to reach the same outcomes.

So let's think a little differently about what we mean by disruptive technology in education. It is illustrative to think of other industries as examples of where genuine disruption has occurred.

**The Motor Industry**: The most famous example, perhaps, is Henry

Ford's innovation of the manufacturing production line to mass-produce motor cars. Until this innovation, craftsmen worked on a single vehicle, and time was taken to make a machine of quality. The motor car was a luxury item. Ford's production line allowed the assembly of many cars speedily, efficiently and at a low cost. He was able to expand the marketplace by producing a quality, but affordable, motor car. Technological change here involved a **change to the system of production**. The disruption occurred because the market expanded, demand was increased, and the cost of vehicles was dramatically reduced, undercutting those manufacturers who were producing luxury products for the wealthiest customers.

**Digital Photography:** Kodak was a company with over a century of dominance in the photographic film industry. It made photographic film, and the camera equipment which could use the film to produce photographs. It was one of the most recognisable brands in the world. Kodak engineer Steve Sasson actually invented the first digital camera in 1975. However, Kodak failed to produce a digital strategy until 2004. While they had produced a digital camera, and even a system by which digital images could be placed on a disk, uploaded to a PC, and then printed at home as early as 1990, the company had failed to recognise that the analogue film and development process was becoming old hat. The company, as an incumbent in the photography market, and affected by its history and previous multi-billion dollar success, was in denial, leading to an analogue mindset regarding photographic film. A host of competitor companies embraced digital technology which allowed a person to take unlimited pictures, upload them to a computer, store and share the images, all at no cost. In the ten years between 1993 and 2003, more than 100,000 Kodak employees had been made redundant worldwide. The technological innovation was the digital camera – produced by Kodak themselves, but never fully realised and utilised within a strategy. The disruption was to the process of photograph production and publishing. This made for a speedier and easier process of achieving results, and was absolutely free of charge to the user as long as they had a digital camera and a computer. Kodak filed for bankruptcy in 2012. After 131 years in business and, at height, more than 90% market share of camera and film sales, with $10 billion dollars of sales by 1981, a firm on which hundreds of thousands of people relied for their livelihoods crumbled: a human tragedy behind all the business statistics (Source: Lucas, H.C. Jr *The Search for Survival. Lessons from Disruptive Technologies*, 2012).

**Dictator Governments:** Well, I know – this is not exactly an industry or a business. Having said that, there are plenty of people in our schools who do not want to see themselves as being involved in an industry or a business either. The Arab Spring of 2011 was an incredible and unprecedented time of political change, and for the dictatorships of the Arab region, were certainly disruptive. After decades of dictatorship rule from Bahrain to Libya, and from Egypt to Tunisia a social media phenomenon swept the dictators from power. Usually, regime changes of this type would be localised and led by politicians or military leaders. The force for change in these countries was ordinary people who had had enough, and who used social media to co-ordinate gatherings and protests. By posting images of abuses by the state on Facebook, tweeting on Twitter, and linking Twitter to Facebook, news spread. When, in Egypt, the government blocked Twitter and Facebook, a telephone number provided by Google enabled Egyptians to post voicemails which were then translated to tweets. The attention of the world focused on the Middle East, and in January, 2011 Zine el Abidine Ben Ali, the dictator of Tunisia, fled the country after 23 years of ruling a police state. This provided a catalyst for Egyptians, 30,000 of whom showed up at a mass protest in Alexandria on 25 January. Within a week a new government took over in Egypt, and by 11 February President Mubarak resigned and left Cairo. The knock-on effect in other countries has been rather difficult to attribute solely to social media. NATO assisted rebels in Libya to remove Gaddafi, and the Syrian horror is still in progress as I write. However, the initial impetus in the region can be traced to the social media, used innovatively and relentlessly. Social media is the technology, while the disruption comes from mass mobilisation and immediacy of information which cannot be controlled by the incumbent power.

**Books:** Now here is a subject which I am sure is close to every reader's heart. Are you reading a physical copy of *Classroom In The Cloud*? Perhaps this is on a kindle or other e-reader? Did you purchase this copy via Amazon, or did you head down to your local Waterstones? Earlier I mentioned the disruption to Borders (and indeed every other book retailer), from Amazon. Borders filed for bankruptcy in 2011, and subsequently went into liquidation. What is interesting is that Amazon set up in 1995, and the two main book store chains in the USA, Borders and Barnes & Noble opened their online stores within three years. Yet Amazon, with no prior retail experience took off while the others did not. Analysis of why points to the fact that the major retailers were not convinced that online sales would catch on. Both were in a state of some denial, believing in the experience of browsing and shopping for books which customers would value. Amazon has now become a major internet department store, and gone way beyond books. Between 2005 and 2010, Amazon's retail sales of all goods increased from $8bn a year to $36bn a year. During the same period, B&N increased from $5bn a year to $6bn. Borders sales fell from $4bn to around $2bn a year.

The retail sales figures are interesting for a number of reasons. First, the Amazon figures show that they are in fact a disruptive player. They have not been one-hit wonders, but retain an awe-inspiring focus on carnivorously gobbling up a range of industries. Their willingness to adapt and chase the next target is firmly based, however, in believing that people prefer to buy online, and also that people want a vehicle to sell online without the overheads attached to normal retail. Secondly, I am interested in the difference between Borders and Barnes & Noble. Borders failed to develop their business sufficiently to remain competitive. Eleven thousand of its employees lost their jobs as a consequence. That means 11,000 families previously reliant on this business. Barnes & Noble have caught on a little. They have developed their online presence, invested in internet books, hired internet specialists at the expense of book buyers, and seen sales increase modestly. They have remained true to themselves, but adapted where necessary, and are still in business. They have also capitalised on the failure of Borders in the USA to be the main seller of the physical book, for which there is still a large market. Between 2002 and 2007, book sales actually increased in the USA by more than $1bn a year. In 2010, sales had fallen slightly, but there were still $15.3bn of book sales during that year. People do like a traditional book. They do like the physical purchase. But they like to browse and shop online in their dressing gown while eating their cornflakes as well!

Innovations in the way in which we purchase books have been very interesting, as they hit the industry on a number of levels. First of all, there are the bricks and mortar bookstores, from major chains to corner shop sellers. Their prices take into account the real estate, storage, stock management and staff salaries necessary to run their business. Secondly, the publishing industry is disrupted. They no longer have as much demand for physical books, and need to decide on cover price knowing that online sellers can undercut this. They need to decide on whether to publish as an eBook, paperback or hardback. They need to pay sufficient royalties to the author to stop the author self-publishing, where royalties can reach as much as 70%. Authors, too, have been disrupted. They need to be more technically aware. They need to promote their work differently. Everyone is an author now, and it is harder for quality work to be recognised and get to publication. The whole industry is in turmoil. The technology here is the internet, but the disruption has come in many forms, from the way we write, to the way we publish, to the way we distribute, and the way in which people experience buying. We have even looked at the physical product – the book – and have reinvented it in a more user-friendly format. While this has not necessarily changed the experience of reading fundamentally, it has certainly changed the experience. I have a Kindle. I don't like using it as much as a physical book. I still take physical books on holiday with me. I am not won over. I have a deep affection for the feel, smell and experience of turning pages. However, I read an enormous amount which is published on the internet on my iPad. I use the iBooks app when I do not have a physical book with me. The multi-function nature of the iPad means that I always have it with me, and so can use it more readily. I do not have to remember to pack it. My reading habits remain conservative, but they have certainly changed.

The above examples draw heavily on Hank Lucas's book, referenced above. I make no apology for this. He examines in far more detail these industries, and others which have faced disruption, and seeks solutions for those industries which may yet face disruption of their own. What I would now like to examine is the lessons we can learn from these industries, and relate them to education. Specifically, let us consider education in the UK.

Education, for the purposes of this study, is our industry. It is our business. As a business, it is interpreted in a variety of different ways. Some would have it that education is a right, and that it should be provided free of charge. Others say that the resources which are necessary for a good education demand that it should be paid for. There are many people who see education as a lucrative business from which they can make money for themselves and shareholders. So, it is a complicated business.

Education is also about people. It is about children, young adults, and life-long learners. It is also about teachers being learners as well as being guides and pedagogues. My specific experience is in the education of children and teachers. I have taught in the primary and secondary sectors since 1996. I have some experience of training in corporate environments, but it is our schools which I would like us to focus on, primarily. Our great problem is defining what it is that our schools actually do. It would be wrong to embark on an examination of how our business is facing disruption without agreeing on the goals of our business. However, that is where we hit the brick wall. Education means different things to different people.

The motto of Winchester College is '*Manners Mayketh Man*', and that of my own alma mater, Manchester Grammar School, is '*Sapere Aude!* (Dare To Be Wise!)'. The school of which I am currently Head, King's Ely, strives for '*Courage, Energy, Integrity*'. Soham Village College, my local maintained academy in Cambridgeshire has an aim of '*Achieving Excellence With Care.* League tables do not appear in any of these. They are about morality, compassion, courage, pushing the boundaries, effort, commitment, curiosity and human development. They are about drawing out the best in our young people. In contrast, let us consider what politicians are interested in: PISA table position; league tables; five A*-C at GCSE; transferrable skills; employability; STEM subjects; EBacc; Literacy Hour; Numeracy Hour. Not that these are unimportant, you understand. But these are the measurable, the statistical, the quantifiable and the competitive. They are the worthy and necessary, rather than the inspirational and engaging. They are basics and fundamentals so that boxes can be ticked and targets can be achieved. They are dull and joyless, but schools are exciting and joyful places. Walk past a primary school at playtime, and hear the cacophony of children having fun. Sit in the audience of a school drama production, or observe a fixture against a rival school from the touchline, or yes, even sit in a good lesson and see the banter, challenge, humour, interaction and friendship between teacher and students as they learn together. This defines schools, and education. Education is about engagement, fun, excitement, wonder, curiosity and personal achievement within a personal context.

I am pleased to say that I think business is catching up with this while politicians lag behind. Businesses, after all, are also about people. While they want clever employees, which is demonstrable by achievements in public examinations, they above all want engaging employees who are interesting and interested, courteous, agents of change, resilient, influencers, open-minded and not only skilled, but adaptable to learning new skills. It is with this in mind that schools themselves have been changing in recent years. A focus on the necessary skills of independent learning, assessment for learning, learning to learn, metacognition, and the adaptability to change have all become features of the curriculum alongside the traditional learning habits aimed at knowledge retention for the purpose of passing examinations. This is to be welcomed, as the tyranny of the examination, and 'teaching to the test' has been countered by teachers who want children to be engaged in the learning process, and wish to enjoy their own jobs more.

It is this focus on collaborative and independent learning skills which have helped establish the UK's reputation overseas for excellence in creativity and adaptability in our education system. Students from overseas have come here in increasing numbers to boarding schools and universities, attracted by our demand that students be inquisitive, apply learning, and develop their own theories. We welcome the question and challenge of the teacher and other learners which in some cultures would be anathema. We have also championed the idea of the individual learner developing at his or her own pace, and in his or her own way. This has led to broad curricula in our schools which, while presenting the problem of giving each subject sufficient time for skills and knowledge to develop, has also added variety, choice and opportunity which enables children to develop in a whole host of ways. New subjects have been added to the school curriculum which would not have featured a couple of decades ago: film and media studies; psychology; textile design; food technology; music technology.

Along with developing one's own portfolio of subjects which is personal and distinctive, this also has produced a focus on the ways in which children learn, and the need for them to develop at their own pace. Investments have been made in learning support departments, and in gifted and talented programmes. Differentiation of task has been a focus of lesson planning as teachers are encouraged to focus on the learning needs of each and every student. Within a class of 30 children, this is difficult. The task of lesson delivery has become more thoughtful and reflective, but is also much more difficult from the point of view of the teacher. Educators seek solutions to these problems, and online technology presents us with a number of options.

So, back to the business of education. Our business is political. Our business is expensive. Our business serves an enormous range of customers in a host of different ways. Our business, crucially, does not have one product or clearly defined objective that everyone can agree with. Education means different things to different people. As such, those leading education have an opportunity to re-think it, re-position it, and to innovate. Meanwhile, those education leaders whose views are intractable and narrow have a problem. They face the incumbent's dilemma in that they are ideologically wedded to a view of what 'good' education is, and they are fundamentally opposed to anything which threatens their view. But education has a long history of trends, movements, and political interference in the UK. Now that it exists on a global platform, UK education is subject to the interpretations of a host of different cultures and ideas. Because it exists on a global platform, it draws the acute interest of politicians and business leaders.

There is a paradox here: while our politicians and business leaders extol the virtues of the UK education system as producing the creative, innovative, thoughtful and collaborative minds which make Britain great, they are also critical of the level of competitiveness when it comes to our numeracy and literacy standards in comparison to other countries. They are critical of the lack of skills with which our young people leave school. They demand higher examination results, more diversity in the skills needed for the workplace, and greater technological awareness. This leads to a demand that we focus on STEM subjects and stop messing around with the nice to haves. Why is this?

Frankly, and unsurprisingly, it is because all schools in the UK are not equal. In 1997, Tony Blair swept to power with a landslide victory, and his mantra, "Education. Education. Education". He promised to invest in the nation's schools in an unprecedented way, and he delivered. This stemmed from the belief that our education system was not serving our children well. In the words of his lieutenant, Andrew Adonis:

> Across much of England, comprehensives were palpably and seriously failing. I regarded this not just as an educational crisis but a social and economic crisis, too, since the poor standard of education of school leavers was so obviously at the heart of England's problems at large. I saw failing comprehensive schools, many hundreds of them, as a cancer at the heart of English society.

Andrew Adonis,
*Education, Education, Education: reforming England's Schools (2012).*

The subsequent intervention of political drive and the injection of vast quantities of money into our education system did an enormous amount to address and improve standards in many schools. The National College for School Leadership, Building Schools for the Future, and the Academies Programme transformed school leadership, school buildings, and the attitudes and results of benefiting schools and communities. But it was not enough, and the money ran out. Adonis' vision of creating state schools which could offer an education on a par with the private sector in the UK was borne out in some flagship academies. The independent sector was affected by strong maintained schools, free of charge, on their doorsteps at exactly the time that they themselves were increasing fees astronomically, and lost the assisted places scheme which Labour abolished in 1997, and which had previously made private education more affordable for many parents (including my own). The impact was not to eradicate the social problems which Adonis longed to address, but in fact to level the playing field for the best schools, while reinforcing the two-tier system which existed in English education. There were still, and are still, failing schools, lack of ambition, low standards and lack of investment. The Coalition government, bereft of the funds lavished by their predecessors, have sought to continue those aspects of the academies programme which sought to address standards through rigorous inspections, the enabling of free schools, and the extension of numbers of academies. However, this government also appears to be fixated on competitiveness, skills and traditional educational values, interpreted as 'rigour'. The impact has been a narrowing of what is valued in education.

So, there are confusing messages about. We need to interpret these in a way which is helpful, and lead our schools in spite of the political and economic storms which rage beyond our gates. Leadership is vital. We must focus on what we believe is in the best interests of our children, and in the survival of all that we value and can be proud of in our education system. What is it that really does distinguish us as a country, and produces excellence? Let us not focus on the difficulties, but seek to accentuate the positives. In doing so, we can marry these areas to the disruptive technologies, and change from incumbents of an outmoded system to become the leaders and innovators of a new system. We can seek to do what we have done for centuries, and roll with the times. We can re-think our schools and education system in order to cope with the new technologies and continue to educate children well.

Children will need educating despite the changes in the political, economic, cultural or social landscape. Children will need educating whether they are holding chalk and slate, pen and paper, or an iPad. The question is, who will educate them, and how? Can we name the disruption facing us? Let me offer you some alternatives:

- The changing role of the teacher
- The changing purpose of school
- The changing purpose of education
- Online tuition, assessment and research tools
- The changing education marketplace
- The changing demands of educational leadership

Some of the above are inter-related. Some may not be disruptions at all, but merely evolutionary changes which we are in the throes of as we speak. Some are the natural consequences of disruption, rather than the disruptive innovation. Let us look more closely:

## The changing role of the teacher

In the UK, I would argue that the days of a teacher being the 'sage on the stage' have long gone. This type of teacher has been replaced by the 'guide on the side'. In some ways, this makes our teachers distinctive from much of the rest of the world.

Now, it is important that a teacher knows what they are talking about. A teacher is not simply a facilitator who points a learner in a particular direction and opens new doors when the learner finds it difficult to take the next step. This is certainly part of the role of the British teacher, however, stemming from the recent focus in developing the independent learner. It would be difficult to argue that this was not always the case. The best teachers have always elicited curiosity from their pupils and brought them to an understanding of how to make an intellectual journey on their own. This is the 'leading out' which comes from the Latin *educare*. However, in times gone by a great proportion of the class time would be directed by a teacher at the front of the classroom, demonstrating, relating and challenging whole classes or even drilling them in acts of memorisation. In some cultures, this prevails, but the inspection culture and emphasis of AfL, Learning to Learn and personalised learning have demanded that the facilitation techniques of our teachers have been developed and are more highly valued.

Teaching has changed in other ways as well. The teacher is no longer simply expected to be a subject specialist, turning up to take their history, geography or mathematics classes, and then going home after a good day's work instructing. The modern British teacher spends an inordinate amount of time tutoring. This tutoring function combines both the pastoral stewardship and academic guidance of individual students. While a tutor may still have a single age form group or a vertical gang of tutees of different ages, the focus is undoubtedly on the further care and welfare of the individual student, supporting them through the trials of adolescence as they make decisions about their future academic path. This is a highly developed and time-intensive skill. It brings teachers into closer contact with parents, social workers, and their colleagues in a context which is not purely academic. The children benefit from an advocate, carer and academic mentor of their very own. While schools have differing structures for academic and pastoral guidance, and while pupils of different ages require a slightly different 'service', this tutoring function is performed by teachers in some ways more intensively than the teaching of their academic subject. It has become an important part of the job of a teacher, and one which presents challenges if we are to countenance blended or online learning.

One way in which we may be seeing a concerning change to the teaching job description is the erosion of the other duties which a teacher is now expected to perform in the area of co-curricular activities. The English teacher who also directs the school play, or the head of chemistry who takes a camp to the Lake District and coaches a football team still exist in our schools. However, they are becoming rarer. Even in the independent sector, which has always had a long tradition of this kind of teacher activity, the administrative and time-consuming nature of the job beyond the classroom, coupled with pastoral demands, and the accountability required at examination time, have eroded goodwill or simply mean that these exciting and rewarding extras are a bridge too far for the teacher seeking a work/life balance. Such activities are therefore either diminished in frequency and scope, are offered by instructors and coaches paid part time for this specific function, or fall to a dwindling pool of 'schoolmasters and schoolmistresses' who see it as a beneficial and necessary part of their job. Even these latter can become resentful of the fact that the load seems always to be borne by their small group.

All of the above shifts in the role of the teacher are, I would argue, positioning our schools in a place which plays into the hands of disruption. They create the atmosphere of individual focus on each child, and erode the necessity of the teacher as instructor and knowledge-giver. The teacher now becomes a carer, an engager, and a specialist in stewardship, rather than in academic subject. This suits some, but not all. An instructional model which is highly personalised, runs at the pace of the individual student, with interventions from specialists, both academic and extra-curricular allows for a different kind of school.

## The changing purpose of school

If we regard school as a building, with bricks and mortar, classrooms, playgrounds and assembly hall, we can think through our issue in a very radical way. If we think of school as an experience for the pupil, our thought processes can be no less radical, and yet the outcome will be very different. By regarding school as both a physical environment and the experience, we can begin to see that the changing role and expectation of the teacher, caused by innovations in the ways in which we want our children to learn (independently and as individuals) can lead to a different interpretation of 'school'.

In the new educational world we now inhabit, teachers are developing different skill sets. They are either academic experts who can inspire in a classroom, or pastoral mentors who are developing exceptional listening and diplomatic skills as they steward young people and their parents. In addition, they may be specialist coaches and instructors. It is becoming increasingly difficult to perform all of these functions to an expert level, and yet we currently often expect teachers to do so. By overloading teachers as we are, we do a disservice to them. But we also do a disservice to our children and their parents, as we do not develop expertise, and we short-change them with tired, over-worked staff who sometimes operate outside their comfort zone. This damages the experience of school.

There are still those teachers who can be the wonderful schoolmistress – inspirational in the classroom, on the netball court and good company on an art trip to the Tate – and such teachers are like gold dust because they enrich a school. Until now, there was not really any other conceived way of deploying staff other than to double up the tasks of academic teacher and pastoral tutor, while asking staff, through goodwill or paltry pay enhancements, to perform the extras. It is just too expensive to employ an army of specialists. However, if we could dramatically increase the ratio of pupils to teachers in some way, this would be more affordable. Blended learning offers a potential solution to a staffing costs crisis, with the added advantage of being able to deploy teachers and coaches in such a way that the expertise is utilised in exactly the right places. This makes for a narrower focus of expertise for the teacher, but arguably also an enhanced experience for the pupil. I say arguably because that 'gold dust' teacher might no longer see the child in the pastoral, academic and co-curricular contexts which promote a deep knowledge and understanding of the child. We need to keep this last point in mind as we think through the shape which our school of the future might take.

## The changing purpose of education

In our history, the education of our children has had many key drivers, from promoting religion, to developing a 'Renaissance Man'. The Victorians and Edwardians faced problems of relieving poverty, and producing a civil service and military top brass capable of running an empire. Subsequent governments sought to organise our home workforce into white and blue-collar workers. The past 150 years have in many ways lost touch with the original purposes of education and have treated schools as functional institutions focused on the social and economic needs of the nation, rather than the needs of children themselves.

Earlier in the chapter I discussed the values and mission statements of different schools. We see that the purpose of education is different for each individual and organisation. This being the case, it is impossible to boil down to one direction. However, what is emerging is a sense that schools are gravitating more and more towards the notion that they should get the very best out of each and every individual student, while the country wants its schools to produce graduates with the skills and personal qualities to function flexibly and successfully in a global economy.

There is now an acknowledgement and acceptance that individual learners differ in their learning styles and aptitudes. There is no place any longer for a 'one size fits all' education system. It would be seen to be anachronistic. If this is the conclusion which we are reaching as a nation (and we are not

LIBRARY, UNIVERSITY OF CHESTER

alone in this), then we need to seize the day and reform our school system. Ken Robinson, in his books *The Element* (2009) and *Out of Our Minds* (2001) has been advocating this for a decade or more, and believes that the time is ripe for a 'new Renaissance' (*Out of Our Minds*, p. 174). I mentioned earlier that it is baffling that despite the enormous popularity of Robinson's theories, nothing has happened to change the system. But perhaps it is not so baffling? The system is embedded. It has needed to change, but attitudes need to change first. The acknowledgement that all people are creative and talented, but that schools must unlock this creativity rather than suppress it, is an idea which now prevails. So, although the purpose of education: to draw out what is good and special in a pupil, is a centuries-old idea, there has needed to be a re-engagement with this of late, and the atmosphere is ripe not only to challenge the system which the Victorians constructed, but to deconstruct it completely. Robinson's ideas are the challenge to the education system which he decries. What they required is the technology to make their impact powerful, and to make their implementation possible. The internet brought Robinson's views to millions through the accessibility of the TED talk he made in Monterey. The use of TED by independent learners as an online learning platform has enabled those who believe in independent learning to spread the word. The way in which his ideas might become reality are surely based in the capability of online learning to blast apart the restrictions to the kind of schooling Robinson envisages, namely" denial, history, resistance to change, mindset, sunk costs and lack of imagination.

## Online tuition, assessment and research tools

The specifics of online and blended learning, and how they might enhance the learning experience and outcomes for children in our schools will be discussed in the following chapter. In this section, I want to make the case for the fact that this is indeed the answer to breaking the Victorian system and re-engaging with the purpose of education which this functional, imperial system impeded.

To begin with, the present system is enormously expensive. Teachers' salaries, National Insurance and pensions account for an enormous tax bill for the UK population, on top of which parents of independent school children pay large fees. In July 2014 a study commissioned by the stockbroker Killick and Co. and carried out by the Centre for Economics and Business Research analysed data on school fees and average earnings over the past 24 years, and found that the rise in independent school fees in the UK had been so dramatic since the 1990s that:

> The average doctor, accountant or professional is not the typical private school parent – at least not any more.

Since 1990, the study found that the average day fee had quadrupled from £2,985 to £12,700 per year, while boarding fees had risen from £6,800 to £28,800 per year on average. The study suggested that spending on teachers' pay had contributed in large part to such a rise.

There are implications for the state sector. With such large fees, and the lack of affordability of our independent schools which this means, many middle class parents who may previously have chosen a private education are seeking either a mixed path of state and private education for their children, or will seek wholly state school provision. This will have an impact upon resources and the staff salary bill in the maintained sector. Teachers in state schools are now often paid comparable salaries to those in the independent sector. In order to keep salary bills down, maintained sector schools will need to compromise in other areas: either curriculum breadth, bricks and mortar resources, or extra-curricular and pastoral provision. This is especially the case in an economy only gradually emerging from a devastating recession.

It means that, if we are to maintain excellence where it exists, alternative methods of delivery or funding are necessary. Funding may well come in the shape of benefactors – either individual or corporate. The Academies programme sought such investment, with some success, although corporate sponsorship of schools requires successful outcomes if the funding is not to disappear very quickly. Independent schools seek, through the setting up of development offices, and the activities of the IDPE (Institute for Development Professionals in Education), to raise funds from alumni for both construction of new facilities and bursaries. These fund-raising initiatives are labour-intensive and far from guaranteed to be successful, or to keep pace with the needs of the school. Development of facilities is one thing. Basic maintenance of buildings which are in some cases centuries old is quite another.

The cost base in a school is in staff and buildings. Staff: pupil ratios vary from 1:6 through to 1:20, depending on the range of activities within a school. Online teachers can reach hundreds of students, or even thousands. Online lectures can allow students to work at their own pace. The face-to-face time, and the necessity of such time, is reduced considerably. Rather than 30 children per classroom, the students can learn anywhere – especially with mobile technology such as smartphones and tablets. In many contexts, these are devices which pupils or their families own already, and so there is relatively little hardware to buy. Software is becoming more and more cheaply available, with the likes of Microsoft offering free use of some student packages in the hope that by becoming confident in the use of Microsoft technology, children will become future customers. From a local or national government point of view, the maintenance, capital project and salary costs to support traditional schools begin to look like money down the drain. It is certainly worthy of further analysis. With creativity, the aspects of a 'good' education which may be threatened alongside such efficiency measures can be preserved by those teachers and school leaders who devise the courses and structures to support online and blended schools.

If we can guarantee the excellence of provision, and more importantly an enhanced provision for students and their families, then the current system is ripe for disruption, and it may well happen very quickly indeed! Already, the smart education and learning market is expected to grow by 20.3% a year to 2017. A study by MarketsandMarkets (a global market research company based in Dallas, Texas that analyses growth areas for investors), predicts that the market is set to grow from $73.8bn (2011 data) to $220bn by 2017. The study reported a growing shift by educational providers from a traditional classroom environment to an automated virtual learning environment. The trend has already brought forth an increased range of technological solutions which, says the report, are being 'rapidly adopted'. Digital textbooks and the test and assessment segments of the market lead the educational content segment with growth rates of 51.6% and 26.4% respectively (Source: *marketsandmarketsblog.com*).

The report makes fascinating reading, including an in-depth analysis of various modes of learning across geographical areas. Currently, North America has the largest market share (60%), and is expected to grow by more than 15% a year, but the biggest opportunities are forecast for the Asia Pacific region due to the significant increase in spending by users as they seek to access the new technologies for learning. The implications for UK schools are obvious: if they are to remain ahead of the game and be seen as exemplary, they will need to take the plunge in one way or another.

Alongside US companies, the UK companies Pearson PLC and Promethean World PLC are named in the report as becoming market leaders, and with such opportunity for investors, it is hard to believe that educational service providers will be promoting traditional products for much longer. Can schools dictate to these providers? Will schools have the courage to follow? Will it, in fact, become necessary to do so? There is even more importance attached to decision making by leaders of schools in such a rapidly changing climate.

# Chapter 4

# Is it learning? The benefits of blended learning for UK schools

Every few hundred years in Western history there occurs a sharp transformation ... society rearranges itself, its world view, its basic values, its social and political structures ... We are currently living through such a transformation.

Peter Drucker, Post Capitalist Society, 1993

D o you remember our duck at the beginning of the book? We were able to see a duck in a wholly new light ... but it was still a duck. It was not really a little yellow dog. The mask did not fool us. What is interesting about the little yellow dog mask, once spotted, is how obvious it becomes. We never thought of the duck's bill in this way before, even though we could see it, and nothing had changed. The duck continues to be a duck.

The duck is my metaphor for education in the UK. Once we view education in a new way, we actually will not change the very purpose of education. We will still educate. But we will have a new perspective and focus.

What may change considerably, however, is the environment for learning: the school. This will trouble some readers who like the familiarity of our present structures, systems and buildings. However, buildings can be used in new ways, structures and systems can be made more elegant and streamlined. It depends very much on how we want to deliver learning. Can we do so in a more exciting, efficient and pleasing way?

Daphne Koller, of the University of Stanford, gave a talk to TED at Edinburgh in August 2012. She began by outlining the difficulty of gaining access to higher education in some parts of the world, such as South Africa, where there simply were not enough places available. She continued by outlining that the costs of college tuition fees in the USA had increased by 559% since 1985, outstripping rising costs of medical care (400%) and consumer goods (200%) during the same period. This, she said, put higher education beyond the reach of many in even a developed nation with fine educational institutions like North America. I have argued that top quality education in UK independent secondary schools is similarly unaffordable for the vast majority, with the consequent knock-on pressures for our maintained sector schools.

Koller quoted *New York Times* journalist Thomas Friedman, writing on May 15, 2012 in that publication: 'Big breakthroughs happen when what is suddenly possible meets what is desperately necessary.'

Koller, and her partner Andrew Ng, who co-founded Coursera, made possible the enrolment of more than 100,000 people on one of Stanford University's first Massive Open Online Courses (MOOC), instead of the 400 students who would normally have taken the course at Stanford. This represented the equivalent of 250 years of traditional teaching to reach such a number of students. Not only that, but his students accessed Ng's course from all over the world.

Coursera was formed with the goal to take the best courses, taught by the best instructors at the best universities, and make them available to everyone around the world for free.

This is an important point, I think, at which to stop and reflect. Koller is talking about university courses from top institutions. These courses require a certain amount of understanding and intellectual maturity to access. Imagine what might happen if a secondary school did something similar!

Analysing the power of this medium for education in the first six months of Coursera's life, 1.5 million people had enrolled on the courses, from 190 countries, and 14 million online course videos had been viewed. In the two years since Koller's TED talk, the number has grown to 22,232,448 enrolments (figure last updated January, 2014), and more than 100 partner universities and other learning institutions offer certificated and authenticated courses.

Coursera is not the only organisation offering MOOCs. The phenomenon of online and blended learning has caught hold extraordinarily quickly in higher education institutions and high schools around the world. Sometimes the speed of such changes is off-putting. Schools can be very conservative institutions. They have a rhythm which is repeated year on year. There are certain annual events and examinations which focus the attention of the institution. Major changes require planning and effort. That means that schools are loath to leap too quickly. The slow-moving nature of change in schools does not lend itself to organisational shift to a blended learning model.

This is potentially very dangerous. In Chapter 5 we will look at how to develop a strategy and a plan to bring about blended learning carefully and without making too many mistakes. First of all, though, let's look at what blended learning actually is, and consider the potential benefits of online and blended learning for secondary schools. Then we will consider some case studies where research demonstrates the actual impact of blended learning on educational outcomes. Next, we consider why we should embrace eLearning as UK schools in the face of the current prevailing conditions.

## What do we mean by blended learning and online learning?

E-learning comes in a variety of forms, many of which are already being explored in our schools, and which are already well established in schools overseas. Blended learning refers to any type of learning which takes place in part in a bricks and mortar school, and partly using online materials which the student can access at their own pace and in their own time in any location. This is not to be confused with online learning (also called e-learning or cyber school), in which all instruction, feedback and assessment takes place away from a traditional school. This is mainly used in business environments to deliver inexpensive training programmes to employees, although there are some virtual schools for K-12 students (kindergarten to high school age).

There are at least six models of blended learning, which differ slightly depending upon resources, timetable constraints, teacher expertise, physical space available and delivery methods. These are:

- Face to Face driver: The learning takes place almost entirely in the classroom, but there are occasional exercises, for instance designed for children who miss a class, or who need to work at a slightly different pace to other students, in which the teacher employs some online strategies in a 'flipped classroom'. The 'flipped classroom' will probably be most familiar to UK teachers. The concept is that learning and instruction happens outside the classroom via online material, and the pupil brings what they have learnt into the classroom for follow-up activities in groups, or with the facilitation of the teacher. This is the standard practice flipped because it reverses the concept of teacher delivering new concepts, and the child going off to perform exercises, write-ups, essays and projects at home in isolation to test and reinforce their learning.
- Online Lab: An entire course is delivered within a bricks and mortar school, but online. Children work at their own pace through the course, and achieve assessment grades along the way as they

complete tasks. These courses are taken alongside the traditional courses, and are either timetabled or taken in the students' own time. For example, at my school, there is a basic computer proficiency course which develops skills in how to use a computer for basic tasks such as email, PowerPoint, spreadsheet design *etc* for which students have a timetabled weekly lesson in their first year of their time in school.

- Rotation: During a course, students rotate on a fixed schedule between online instruction and time face to face with a teacher. This allows a teacher to teach to different classes, reaching more students. It cuts down the face to face instruction time, but the same amount of material is covered, and teaching is more efficient.
- Self Blend: Students take online courses to supplement their usual traditional curriculum courses. For instance, a linguist whose school does not offer a Latin class may take Latin online. An exceptional student who wants to extend their understanding beyond their A-level course in preparation for university interview takes a Coursera course offered online by a university. Alternatively, a school offers a core curriculum and provides its own elective courses online.
- Flex: A school provides almost all of its course content through an online platform, and teachers offer time through seminars and tutorials to support students as and when they need academic guidance and deeper understanding, or indeed if they are falling behind with expected deadlines.
- Online Driver: All courses are delivered online by a teacher and online platform. Students check in when required by attending a school physically, or via email/skype/*etc*

(Source: www.knewton.com/blended-learning/)

What becomes clear considering these methods is the need for consideration of the age-appropriateness of each type of learning. Some are far more suited to secondary, or perhaps only undergraduate, students. However, what is exciting is the flexibility on offer. The possibilities for creating a school's own blended learning strategy, taking into account the skills and abilities of staff and students, are manifold.

## Potential benefits of e-learning

I am very aware in writing this section that readers may come from schools of vastly differing contexts. However, there are wonderful possibilities for raising aspirations in many different types of school through online education. The student who labours in an atmosphere which is not conducive to learning will have a new space of their own. Online learning levels the playing field for many students, and enables schools to develop strategies which can raise the outcomes for students, and the learning temperature of a school community. It is not only the student who benefits. Teachers, too, can gain enormously from the experience.

Let us think about the potential benefits of online learning, and consider, in a 'blue sky' way, what the implications for our schools may be:

## 1. High quality learning and results become possible in areas of traditionally low quality educational provision

With the exception of some parts of Scotland and the Isles, the UK has the benefit of having most people close to conurbations. Certainly in comparison to the USA and Australia, there is less need for virtual instruction models which serve children on very remote farms, for instance. This difference does mean that we have not perceived the need before such countries, which might place us at a disadvantage. By the end of 2010, 1.5 million US children were engaged in wholly online learning, representing 3% of the total number of children in the US public school system.

> In rural school districts, online learning is not simply an attractive alternative to face-to-face instruction, but increasingly becoming a lifeline to basic quality education. (Picciano and Seaman, 2009)

So let us consider a small British rural secondary school to which students must travel long distances. Such a school may not have the breadth of curriculum which is available elsewhere, or the quality of instruction because it is harder to attract staff to such a remote area. Due to low numbers on roll, the investment in school buildings, facilities and resources has been pretty basic. Through online provision, resource funds can be reallocated by the school leaders to areas most needed in supporting face to face learning, and teacher time can be directed at subject areas where expertise exists. Schools can decide which classes or individual students would benefit from different forms of learning, and can decide how much time is invested in creating their own materials, and how much should be accessed from other providers.

In schools which are failing inspections, children with the will to learn may do so in their own time, free from the distractions of the poor behaviour of others, and with access to quality instruction. They will benefit from the 1:1 instruction of staff who can offer time to guide.

## 2. Greater range of courses available

The new GCSE and A-level specifications which will be coming in from September 2015 will be higher on core content. This will require extra teaching time in certain core subjects, to the detriment of other courses and activities which need to make way for the proposed changes. By devising a suite of online courses alongside core content, and bringing in electives, children with diverse interests and desire to learn can access a wider range, at a pace which can allow them to achieve. Curriculum time is gained for the core content, and as these subjects, too, may be able to offer online courses in a flipped classroom, they may not, in fact, need the contact time which currently threatens other subjects and consigns them to 'also-ran' status.

### 3. Home schooling facilitated

There are two points to be made here. First of all, schools may enter into arrangements with parents who wish to home school their children, and offer supplementary skills and course content which can develop the breadth of education available, while achieving some quality control. Secondly, those parents who currently pay for a tutor to give their child an advantage, or to address a shortfall from difficulties experienced in the normal classroom, may find that online instructional courses addressing key skills could be made available by the school for free without parents feeling that they are paying through the nose, and without teachers having to spend break and lunchtimes providing interminable clinics.

### 4. More access to qualified teachers in shortage subjects

This speaks for itself. In certain subjects, or in certain geographical locations, some subject specialists are very thin on the ground. This presents schools with recruitment problems, but also with problems of cover when they do have a specialist who is incapacitated. An online course taught by a strong specialist not bound by geographical location is an attractive solution.

### 5. Flexible hours for teachers

The strong teacher away on maternity leave, or having to work part-time because of child care problems could be liberated by developing a suite of online courses which could either be delivered in her school, or indeed could be sold to schools seeking to buy an online package. The working parent may in this way develop an income stream which enables more flexible working. The school may save money on covering maternity, or extra part-time staff.

### 6. Specialised schedules

Some students are exceptional in other fields, such as sport or music. Some are involved in professional theatre or film. For children whose lives and talents demand unusual schedules, this allows them more freedom and flexibility to participate in both mainstream school and also their field of expertise. While competing or performing away from home, these students can remain in touch, and indeed acquire the balance and personal organisation which may help them achieve greater levels of success in their specialism.

### 7. School collaboration over courses

In certain locations, or within partnerships of schools, collaboration over courses can be developed. Teachers will gain from sharing best practice with colleagues in another school, learning new methods from partner schools overseas, and introducing these methods to their classes in order to diversify the children's learning experience. Where skills gaps occur in one partner school, they may be supplemented elsewhere. In modern foreign languages, for instance, a school may offer German, French and Spanish in its mainstream, and have an options structure which limits opportunities to develop dual linguists at GCSE and A-level. By partnering with colleagues elsewhere, the teaching of Italian, Russian and Chinese may be possible, and the range of options can be extended for the best linguists. Also, a school which does not have sufficient resources or facilities to provide laboratory practical experiments may benefit from observing a filmed practical from another school which has access to the materials and facilities required.

## 8. Students move at their own pace

The joy of an online course is that a student can really move at his or her own pace. They can pause or replay the teacher. Little knowledge checks can be added periodically to reinforce the learning, and with some software can also give instant feedback to develop understanding. The student may email questions to the teacher which may receive real-time answers if both are logged in at an agreed time.

## 9. Assessment made easier and promotes learning

Submissions of work for assessment at different times from the students can allow teachers to mark at their own pace as well. Many assessment tasks can be set which can be peer marked, or electronically marked, so freeing teachers from this burden, but allowing them to sample and analyse work in order to refine the focus of future lessons where there becomes a clear need for reinforcement.

## 10. Courses beyond school level for the brightest students

Online courses proliferate in Higher Education already. Many schools have been extending very bright sixth formers through the Open University's online or distance learning courses for some years. The number and range of the courses now available from institutions worldwide, and in many cases free of charge, offer extension and enrichment opportunities which not only deepen a student's understanding and demonstrate to a future university their competence and commitment, but also develop and embed the very independent learning habits which make these young people attractive as undergraduate students in the minds of university admissions tutors.

## 11. Teacher training opportunities

It is becoming clear that, even in the online driver model, the excellent teacher is still necessary. In most of the blended learning models, teachers are required to work slightly differently, develop their practice, or fine tune their existing skills. Schools which invest in their staff and offer them support as the blended revolution takes hold will reap the rewards, and their children will benefit enormously.

There are all these potential benefits, but what about the student's experience of school? One of the most fundamental issues which I can perceive causing us to hold back from taking the plunge into blended learning on a large scale is whether the learning experience is in fact enhanced, and whether anything may be lost or eroded which our current schools offer.

Earlier we discussed the need for children to be engaged in their learning. It is not enough to put a computer or smartphone in front of a teenager, and then assume that he will be engaged. If anything, many teenagers would feel more than a little patronised by such an approach. I recently interviewed two ex-pat children who had been living in Shanghai for four years. The family (originally from Liverpool) was relocating back home to the UK for two reasons. One was because the father had received a promotion, but the main reason was that the parents were both worried that their sons now did all of their work at school on an iPad. The boys themselves had been complaining that teachers were not showing them how to use other devices, and they were also worried that, when they took iGCSEs, they would be unable to write the papers efficiently enough due to lack of practice with a pen. My own school was about to launch our BYOD initiative to parents, and here was a family whose school had issued iPads to all, and who were critical of the narrowness of the education on offer.

I was surprised, but also pleased to have gained this brief insight into a possible future which my own school, and many other UK schools, may have inadvertently been about to create. It demonstrated the importance of engaging children in the learning process, and giving them variety of methods to learn and to create. This is possible, of course, with online education, just as it is possible with traditional methods. It is a salutary lesson, however, that we should know what we are doing and plan carefully a host of mobile tools rather than rely on one type of device, used inappropriately and unadventurously by teachers.

So, we need to consider before spending so much time, energy and money on facilitating online education what the actual benefits really are, and whether the learning tools make a genuine impact, or are in fact nothing more than an extra tool in the teacher toolbox.

So far I have outlined some evidence from the USA which outlines the growth of online learning in both Higher Education and K-12 contexts. There is a growing body of evidence from the US, because it has embraced online learning whole-heartedly. The social, political and economic history of the American online learning experience is helpful in understanding why this was the case. However, it may be helpful to examine a variety of other overseas examples of the critical analysis of actual action research by teachers, much of which is available in another book published by John

Catt, *Learning in a Digitalized Age. Plugged in, turned on, totally engaged?* (2014), edited by Lawrence Burke.

Burke has assembled a number of contributions from teachers and academics around the world, and seeks to find a critically informed answer to the question of how successful learners will be in the digital age. The book reflects the dramatic impact, not only on learning and teaching, but on the human experience. Nobody can fail to agree, having read this work, that life and education have changed dramatically. In his own chapter of the book, *Heretical Views from a Digitally Centric Universe*, Burke warns about the folly of uncritically following the mythology that technology might usurp the role of the teacher. He questions whether in fact there has been any conclusive evidence whatsoever that the plethora of devices have in fact created deeper learning in any conclusive way. He also raises concerns about the neurological effect of technology on young developing brains. Not that Burke thinks we should dismiss devices as tools to learning. He merely wants some sort of certainty that its effects are genuinely beneficial before we all follow the crowd, the publishing houses, Apple and the eLearning evangelists without questioning the damage that may be done to individual children, or the wider impact on society of living our lives through technology. His is a genuine question of ethics. He exhorts teachers, parents and school leaders to act in the best interests of children by ensuring that they are appropriately informed.

For our purposes, then, schools should seek an appropriate response. Here I summarise some of the case studies in the book, and reflect on how our school leaders might use this information in their own individual contexts:

**Lisa Martin, Founder of O-MUN (Online Model United Nations), Jordan**
Lisa's article, and her experience, focus on the revelatory experience of her development of an online Model UN as a debating platform between children of different countries, originally devised as a once-per-month activity. It depends on a Blackboard Collaborate online classroom and a Facebook-driven social media network. Beginning with 20 students, it has grown to five monthly debates; a Facebook community of more than 2000 students; a leadership team spanning 20 countries; a middle school programme; a university level programme; and several national programmes in countries as diverse as Turkey, Singapore, Palestine and France.

> When I started O-MUN ... I knew it would be a great debate platform ... and a place to engage in all manner of topics related to international relations. What I didn't know is what I would learn as an educator and how that would change my very concept of learning and teaching.

This is promising, from my point of view. Here is a teaching experiment in online education which has grown like Topsy into an international phenomenon which has changed the perpetrator's entire perspective.

Martin began her model UN club in her high school, and opened her online classroom for her six or seven delegates to set up a first mock debate. Word got out via social media, and students interested in the concept from around the world began logging on. Her two-hour test of an online debate became a 19-hour social media phenomenon of continuous worldwide student engagement. Excited by the educative experience and potential, Martin shared the experiment with a teacher in Singapore and began to develop it, only for her for-profit school in the USA to shut down the programme and bring in lawyers as it sought to gain financial advantage from it themselves. Martin left her job, and went to teach in the Middle East.

Let us think about this. Here was a teacher with an innovative idea which was proving itself to be exciting. But as an employee of a for-profit school, she had no ownership of her concept, and the educative purpose was superseded by the alternative motives of the business. This is an important factor for us to contemplate. In UK schools, how many initiatives from individual teachers will be allowed freedom to develop if they either go against the grain of the institution in which the teacher works, or might increase profile or opportunity for the school itself? Who owns the intellectual property of an online educational initiative: the school or the teacher? Will teachers seek to develop a potential online business from the lessons they devise and become free agents, or will schools need to contract them in such a way that the school owns the rights to the fruits of their labours? It is very hard, writing these questions, not to begin to colour my writing with my own value judgements on teachers' intellectual property versus the school's need, as a business, to thrive and flourish. The scale of online phenomena, and the possibility for a school to exploit this potential scale for financial gain, pose very important ethical questions for us as school leaders. We may find that our former ethics of how schools and teachers operate are challenged by the potential of what we might achieve.

Martin faced further difficulties in her new school in the UAE, so left that job as well, and waited over a year before she re-launched O-MUN in order that her former employers were unable to capitalise on her idea. She had a clear contract with them, and this helped her. After the summer of 2011, O-MUN took off. Martin says that what is lost from a real MUN debate (face to face engagement of students and expensive overseas visits once every year or two), is more than compensated by the diversity of student possible, the frequency and range of debate, and the ability of students who would never otherwise have been able to travel to a real MUN event overseas to participate. They benefit, but the experience for all is enriched by their views, which otherwise would never have been heard and taken into account. This gives the entire exercise a greater integrity. This has led to an O-MUN mission to democratise and diversify the MUN programme to any student with an internet connection.

> O-MUN's online incarnation of a traditional academic programme
> taught me that most of the great things we do in classrooms face
> to face can be done online, and that the power of the technology
> can drive learning, personal fulfilment and community in new and
> unexpectedly wonderful directions.

As well as learning about the potential of an online programme, Martin
also reveals what she learnt about herself as a teacher. First of all, she found
that her digital presence on Facebook, which was necessary to facilitate
the programme, opened her up to the worldwide community which her
programme served, making her much more mindful of her digital footprint as
a teacher. Living this gave her a greater awareness of the realities of life for her
students, and a deeper appreciation of how she as a teacher, and her students,
needed to be mindful of the portrayal of themselves in such a capacity. Are
we, as school leaders, wholly comfortable that the teachers in our schools will
have the professionalism to engage appropriately online with students? What
safeguards will we need to put in place? Such considerations already sound
restrictive, don't they? Actually, should we allow the teachers their freedom
on the understanding that they will be far more likely to regulate themselves
in this context as they become more aware of the online world? It is, after all,
the reality of the way in which many of their students communicate and live.

Secondly, Martin found that the sense of togetherness which is felt by a
teacher and class when things go well in a class-based lesson – the real stuff
of teaching! – is magnified when in a virtual community. There is something
more powerful and honest about the openness of such a community than
many relationships in school. She puts this down to the fact that often school
is a locked down place for students. It is not like real life because of the barriers
which conventions and formality constructs. Those moments of togetherness
which a class and teacher share are powerful because there is a relationship
between them. There is an intimacy. The openness of the online forum in a
virtual classroom creates a sense of community. Martin finds this exciting.

Again, we see that the conventions of the traditional school: modes of
behaviour, dress codes, deference to teachers as authority figures *etc* may
be challenged in an online context. This will not suit every reader. It may
indeed terrify some of us. It is important for us to have our eyes open wide
to such possibilities before embarking upon a programme of our own, and
reflect upon the impact on our own schools.

Thirdly, Martin says that managing the online project felt different from
a traditional classroom, because as a teacher she became the facilitator,
regularly asked students for help, and capitulated on topics where a student
made a good case for doing things differently. In a traditional classroom she
would call the shots more frequently, and depend on student compliance
rather than student initiative or creative engagement to make a lesson work.

Finally, Martin praises the integration of high level academic and leadership skills with technological skills and applications which her particular online programme developed in her students. In addition, the engagement with students from all around the world, and with their values and preconceptions, creates an understanding of life beyond one's own shores which fits children for the global village which they inhabit, and in which they are likely to work and learn in the future. Martin calls this the 'leadership incubator'. This is the very mix of skills which employers in the UK are looking for, and which we vaunt as especially 'British' skills abroad. But let us take note: this particular online programme was an international phenomenon in which UK schools were a small group. Will we be able to claim the high ground on education for very long if we fail to engage with this dynamic way of learning?

> It's not about the technology per se, but what we allow the students to do with it ... it is up to educators and administrators to lay the groundwork to make it happen within education programmes ...
> Tried and true academic programmes with access to technology can transform themselves into beautifully reincarnated and dynamic programmes with renewed relevance and dynamism breathed into them ... student engagement can thrive if appropriate social media activity and leadership structures can be married to academic activities which are both engaging and relevant ... the joy and passion that carried me through my first years of teaching has returned.

## Serge Morissette, extending formal teaching through discussion boards, UAE

Examining the idea that an asynchronous discussion board could be used as a collaborative and interactive tool to assist student learning and reflection, Morissette (a Canadian teacher working in the UAE) focused on the role of the teacher, and whether deeper learning could in fact be achieved. His students took part in traditional lessons, but an online discussion board then allowed them to post comments and communicate about lessons in their own time.

This was an immediate plus to students because they:

- were not limited to short discussion time imposed by the teacher in the classroom.
- could reflect on what they wanted to say.
- had the time to relate what they wanted to say to what had actually happened in the classroom on that day.
- had the time to reflect on what classmates had said.
- could respond without worrying about being cut off by a teacher or fellow student.
- could offer thoughtful help or advice to classmates.
- could choose their own topics to write about.

There was also a record of the discussion, which the students and teacher could examine in order to understand the thought processes involved, and to plan next steps where there were particular difficulties in understanding or mastering concepts. The teacher could also benefit from:

- being able to see most students express themselves rather than just the same few.
- discovering a different dynamism in student discourse given that writers and speakers use different learning styles.
- recognising and rewarding more reflective thinking from students.
- observing a significant increase in supportive and collaborative discourse.
- having the time to respond to each student in a more reflective way.

Morissette observes, however, that many of these benefits could become a pitfall unless there were well thought-out rules established before engagement starts. After all, in a discussion board, the offerings of the students become exposed to more scrutiny, and bullying, control, peer pressure, *etc* may still exist. There are also cultural considerations which affect engagement online as much as engagement face to face or in a classroom forum, although perhaps in different ways.

The students therefore had to be taught how to use the discussion board in appropriate and helpful ways by the teacher. In order that all were engaged in some way, a minimum number of posts was agreed before midnight on the evening of a class, and a higher number of posts would be expected if a student wanted to access higher grade levels for their assessment, which would be partly based on their level of contribution to discussion in terms of number of messages, but also the quality of their engagement, collaborative work, depth of reflection and written fluency. In this way structures devised by a teacher are an important part of the process. It highlights how important it is for the teacher to be thoughtful about such structures. We need to have a strong and yet flexible structure. Students need to understand fully the assessment criteria and how they engage online. But the opportunities for students to participate on a deeper level than in their traditional classroom context is then opened up enormously.

> By the second and third week...students were very much on task and many students' reflections demonstrated how they were taking ownership of their own progress.

Other considerations were important. For instance, the size of a discussion forum. Too many would lead to a vast array of comments which the teacher would be unable to read in its entirety. A class of 20 might actually divide into sub-groups as four or five of them discussed a shared experience or problem. This developed online collaborative or supportive relationships which the teacher could observe in a different context to the classroom setting, and which could be brought into play in class activities later (for instance in going over material again which a small group needed to reinforce). Time management is another issue. A student in school all day may have only limited time to follow up their classwork through the forum, and may have work to do for other classes. This negates, in some ways, the benefits of an online element. However, the separation of teacher and pupils from one another is overcome by the discussion board being accessible at a time convenient to the individual students. Feedback from the teacher is an important consideration as well. If the teacher is able to respond quickly, he may intervene in good time to assist understanding or stop a discussion going in the wrong direction. On the other hand by not intervening, the group may well find its own way out of an intellectual cul-de-sac, which is a rewarding learning exercise as the students find their own solutions and help one another. The solutions they find may even be better ones than those a teacher may impose?

In the last case study, leadership of students was mentioned as an interesting and desirable by-product of the O-MUN programme. In Morissette's discussion forum, students also were seen to develop leadership roles as they took on the mantle of peer mentor or instructor for their classmates. Their own understanding deepened as they demonstrated or explained concepts to their classmates, and their self-esteem was enhanced, as this leadership could later be rewarded or picked up on in the classroom context later by the teacher who observed such a development. This happened more on a discussion board due to the extended time available to the students, which they were unable to have in the classroom.

Teacher time management was an issue which Morissette noted. Discussions which generated more comment naturally took longer for the teacher to read. In addition, at times when the teacher had a lot of work to do during the normal school day, his ability to read comments, and subsequent output, was diminished. This meant that, while comments may have been valuable, they were often not as immediate, reducing the quality of the experience which immediate feedback may have afforded. As a result, teachers need to think carefully about how they manage their time and the expectations of students about teacher intervention in discussion boards. Teachers were necessary to monitor the discussions, because they had the overview of student needs, learning styles and the skills to intervene. Teachers were therefore seen as vital for a discussion board in order to monitor and develop the outcomes of discussions into an evolving instruction programme.

Morissette certainly found that the level of knowledge and understanding of his students deepened considerably as a result of the reflective and collaborative nature of the exercise. This underlines the emerging research on such issues from the likes of Schellens and Valke (2006), and Johnson (2006), who looked at depth of understanding and benefits of collaboration respectively; and also skills such as writing and vocabulary usage grew as a result of students being encouraged to write in the forum, which reinforced the earlier research of Doering (2003). Morissette found that by linking these skills to a summative assessment, the students were incentivised to use the discussion board more. As he introduced this concept, their participation increased markedly.

The students views are interesting to note:
"I love the support I received from my colleagues and teachers."
"I improved my reading, writing and vocabulary."
"I especially liked the fact that the teacher was reading all of my messages."
"I did not feel alone."
"I could see what other students were doing."
"I learned how to apply what I was being taught in the classroom. I learned to be a problem solver by helping others."
They also wrote:
"I did not participate as much as I would have liked to. It is very useful, but very demanding of our time."
"I had to do work for other teachers. The internet was not working, and I was tired after a long day."
"When I was sick, I could not participate for a few days."
So, there is balance in the student experience, the most telling of which is the time pressure or reliance on technology. Nevertheless, there is another example here of students benefiting considerably in their learning, reinforcement of knowledge, and the collaborative nature of online learning to involve all, at their own pace, and to empower those who may previously not have had a voice in a traditional classroom.

## Diane Evans, Michelle Rogers-Estable and Roudaina Houjeir, UAE

Undoubtedly one of the foremost tools associated with the technology revolution is the iPad. While smartphones and tablets produced by other companies than Apple have similar or different capabilities, and in many respects are cheaper, the iPad has claimed a place as the partner to learners due to its versatility and the range of apps which can be employed through it. Many schools have gone down the route of purchasing whole class sets of iPads in order to usher in mobile learning. This extremely expensive option has been rightly called into question. What is there to say that the iPad will remain as the primary tablet in the near future? Will a lack of adaptability of learners be the consequence of an iPad-centric learning system?

In contrast to e-learning and blended learning, mobile learning can also take place in a face to face context within the classroom environment. We need to be careful in discussion about iPads that we do not confuse one of many technological teaching tools with the innovations in teaching and learning which we have so far discussed and which impact on the very concept of school. The iPad, however, is in many ways a potential bridge between the classroom use of technology, and the ability of the user of this technology to then learn beyond the classroom in their own time. It is possible that the iPad – as well as other devices – can be the enabler of blended learning, and as such it does require some specific focus. A key definition that may be helpful here is from Rossing *et al* (2012), who define mobile learning as, 'the efficient and effective use of wireless and digital devices and technologies to enhance learners' individual outcomes during participation in learning activities'.

Mobile learning (mLearning) offers educational groups the opportunity to connect and learn outside the walls of the traditional classroom, (Alexander, 2006), and facilitates opportunities for learners to approach education through a variety of different learning styles (Rossing *et al*, 2012). Further research suggests that the iPad produces enhanced engagement in the learner, and this in turn is what leads to deepening understanding, critical thinking and learning outcomes.

The research in the UAE took place in the tertiary education sector, and as such should be seen in this context, with older learners who had acquired more developed independent learning habits and expectations. The researchers sought to examine the impact of the iPad on various forms of learner literacy, based on Bloom:

- **Basic literacy** of the individual to read, write, compute and solve problems in order to function in society.
- **Critical literacy** of the individual to think critically through logic and reasoning.
- **Digital literacy** of the individual, and their ability to use computers and related technology.
- **Environmental literacy** of the individual to understand ecological principles and the way society effects and responds to environmental conditions.
- **Media literacy** of an individual to analyse, interpret, create and evaluate media messages.
- **Global literacy** of an individual to appreciate the difference and similarities of their own and others' cultures.
- **Creative literacy** of the individual to communicate creatively and effectively through any medium.
- **Health literacy** of the individual to process information and make appropriate health decisions.

This is quite a list, but one which does allow for some measure of learning outcomes. One of Burke's own points in his chapter and his introduction was that there are simply too many variables to appropriately analyse the impact of one piece of technology's impact on learning. However, the use of the above criteria in a system which had so much injection of investment from government gives us an opportunity for some kind of comparative study of the iPad versus a non-iPad system.

By questioning teachers, Rogers-Estable and Houjeir elicited their opinions about their likes and dislikes of the iPad in their teaching. The flexibility of it as a tool for facilitating learning was appreciated. Where there was an app which did not achieve the required function, there were invariably others which could replace it. It offered many educational needs in one small portable device, and teachers could monitor the use of it effectively through using AirPlay. The fact that not only learning tools, but also lecture notes, files and eBooks, plus the ability to retain all notes made, email them and share them made the iPad a very attractive learning tool for teachers and students alike.

The drawbacks to iPads centred around lack of teacher expertise, technical support and distractions to learning. The main barrier to smooth integration of iPads to classrooms were ones of infrastructure in institutions, such as wifi access, while set-up issues caused delays in teaching time when new apps were being installed. Also there were issues with assessing some student work, cost of some apps, and the size of the screen for some activities.

Overall, however, the teachers were in favour of the iPad as a learning tool, and reported enhanced student engagement. There were lots of ideas for the use of iPads created.

Rogers-Estable and Houjeir examined the impact of the mass introduction of iPads into schools through the UAE's federally managed education system. Alongside this introduction of iPads was a large-scale professional development system to support teachers in the use of iPads within their classrooms. The UAE is a wealthy region. Nevertheless, is this an investment worth making? Diane Evans questioned the reasons for the adoption of the iPad as the device of choice, which she felt was not necessarily a strategy developed with education foremost in mind. She points to the 4.5 million sold to education institutions in the US and 8 million to schools worldwide by December, 2013, and writes that some could argue that the introduction in the UAE was 'enforced'.

> Senior managers of the institution displayed a remarkable determination that the iPads would revolutionise the learning experience, using positive terminology with teachers such as 'iCelebrate' to influence perceptions of change.

Her work asks questions about whether the introduction of iPads in education are part of a planned strategic development, or simply an effective piece of marketing either by Apple, or by education providers who wish to be seen as cutting edge.

She outlines the history of Apple's targeting of the education market, from its founding of a division totally focused on education as early as 1979, to the more than 20,000 education apps available on app store by 2012. According to William Isaacson (2012), Steve Jobs is reported by Rupert Murdoch as saying that education would never be transformed by technology, but Jobs did acknowledge that 'the paper textbook business will be blown away by digital learning materials', and that he had an objective to transform the $8 billion a year textbook business by 'digital destruction'.

Continuing to discuss the potential difficulties of learning through the iPad, Evans points out the lack of security felt by students with too much information to analyse. She warns against 'constructivist' learning approaches which rely on student search, and makes a strong case for the role of the teacher in ensuring that methods of research and criticality are developed in order that learners are secure in their findings, and that learning is embedded appropriately. The development of appropriate pedagogy in order to deal with the rapid proliferation of learning apps and access to information is particularly concerning to Evans. She criticises the research of Manuguerra and Petocz, whose findings demonstrate the excellent engagement of students using iPads, but who she dismisses as 'technology enthusiasts and change champions...who gain pleasure from 'playing' with the latest device and will work hard to beat a path through the unknown wilderness...They are not objective critics'.

Evans would prefer 'to make tentative inroads to adapt our approach to our teaching'. She rightly says that engagement through video, multimedia presentations and VLEs has been possible for many years. The iPad neither created this engagement, nor has the monopoly on being able to create students who are engaged. Evans believes only that Apple has, through clever marketing, pushed society's 'must have' button. She is a true sceptic:

> The pedagogical use of iPads in education, known as iPadogogy,..has yet to be fully researched and examined...With no frame of reference, the majority of educators will flounder in a sea of information, inevitably grabbing ideas and practice from the adventurous minority.

Evans' concerns are founded on a belief in the importance of developing learners who will learn what they need to know. She is not convinced that iPads or other constructivist approaches to learning will enable this. Her very idea of 'needing to know', however, is exactly the kind of mindset which technology may be disrupting. Why should anyone need to know anything as long as the person has an ability to analyse, trust and choose wisely from the information available? The very concept of knowing is reactionary. Once someone knows something, it closes their mind to other possibilities. Twenty-first century learning sees a coming together of technological innovation, globalization and a need to understand how people learn. In a world of technological innovation and globalisation, I would argue that technology makes the impossible appear possible, and globalization broadens our horizons, challenges our preconceptions, and promotes a desire to understand more. These promote an open approach to learning, and a more individual reflection of what we know and are curious to know more of.

Julie Lindsay, an Australian educator from Queensland who has taught across three continents, is an absolute advocate of the fact that learning itself is changing:

> In the emerging learning landscape supported by digital technologies, different modes of interacting and sharing provide a multitude of opportunities for everyone. Learning has never been as fluid as now. (taken from 'The Future Is Now. The Future Is Flat' in *Learning in a Digitalized Age*).

Lindsay's experience has developed collaborative learning communities of teachers and students in what she calls 'flat' learning. Developing learning structures which seek collaboration between student and teacher is important to her. This is because she believes that it is imperative in taking learning global and encouraging deeper understanding of collaborative working. Lindsay outlines what she describes as 'connected' learning, in which children working online are not isolated but part of a network of collaboration with their teacher and other students. This allows them to build a PLN (Personal Learning Network). The learners are responsible for developing their own connection strategy, perhaps using social media, and to learn from the interactions they have with their online connections. The online conversation through message boards, twitter, blogging, *etc* is more influential, she says, than traditional textbooks or classroom interaction because learners can develop a greater range of personal interaction, and the conversation is ongoing for them: 'Students are the greatest textbook ever written for one another.'

It is the reason that developing the right network of collaborators is very important. This is where students may be given guidance. 'Flat learning', according to Lindsay, is pedagogy supported by technology which goes beyond instruction and delivery because it eliminates the physical walls of mainstream schooling, and as a consequence connects learners to those of other ages, races and cultures. In so doing, flat learning breaks through stereotypes and promotes global citizenship and understanding. It also promotes active learning, being conducted through the PLN, and therefore requiring engagement and intellectual maturity from the learner. It also requires 'teacherpreneurs': educators who can facilitate connections between schools and learners by seeing the opportunities which may exist for collaboration. Again we see that even in online and international contexts, the teacher is a key component of not only facilitation, but creativity and leadership. This aligns with Ken Robinson's (2001) theory of developing creativity:

> We depend much for our own understanding of the world on the knowledge of other people. We are laced together in networks of knowledge ... The creativity of a culture depends on how open these networks are and how easily we can access the knowledge of other people.

Learning is changing. The possibilities are endless. There is a sense that there is a learning frontier beyond which there is an exciting and dangerous unknown. Those who engage and learn possess a pioneering spirit, and will reap the rewards of daring to learn.

This is surely a revolutionary precipice on which to stand. The 15th and 16th centuries saw a world view challenged, and a subsequent frenzy of exploration, development of political and philosophical ideas, scientific research, and religious conflict. It was a time of an acknowledgement that we did not know everything, and could not know everything. It was an exciting, and very dangerous, time of uncertainty. It was also a time of enormous creativity and daring.

Am I over-stating things? Let us look at what has happened in the past 20 years, or even the past ten years. Can we envisage what will be around the corner, or the world in which our children will begin their working lives? Evans misses the point. She is locked in a world in which concepts of education, pedagogy and knowledge are secure. She is part of an established order which is being rocked, and which is quaking. Where I agree with her is that there is a danger that education may be overtaken by those seeking to gain a pecuniary advantage, pushing their products and leading educators, parents and children down blind alleys. In such scenarios, the function of a school, and its leaders, is to prepare their children for anything. Expose them to technology, but teach them discernment. Expose them to a world view, but teach them who they are, and develop in them a moral compass in order that they might respond appropriately. Expose them to the uncertainty and danger of a world which is shaking, and has monsters at its edge, but equip them to be bold and daring so that they have the wherewithal to sail over the horizon, and meet reality rather than be fearful of myths and legends.

We need to lead our schools with confidence in the face of uncertainty in order to prepare our children. To do so, we need a carefully planned course. We need to be fully equipped, and we may well also benefit from an acknowledgement that the storm is already whipping up. We have already cast off, and there is no benefit in rushing back to harbour.

# Chapter 5

# Setting sail towards a blended learning future: practical strategies

**Change in education is easy to propose, hard to implement, and extraordinarily difficult to sustain.**

Hargreaves and Fink, Sustainable Leadership, 2006

ERHAPS THERE are some readers who have got this far only to be disappointed by the fact that I appear to have entered the realms of hyperbole? To those readers, I say that I am not intentionally over-egging the pudding. I am well aware that the points I raise will have their detractors. I am also well aware that many of our worst fears will not come to pass. There have been many other examples in education of initiatives, technologies or forecasts which have come to nought. This is because we are in a creative business, and those within it are constantly experimenting and theorising. It keeps things fresh, and it serves children well, actually, for all the adults may bluster and disagree, because all that invention, dreaming and debate keeps teachers and politicians passionate ... and that rubs off on parents and their children.

But I make no apologies for writing this book now, because I believe that we are not only on the crest of a wave, but are riding down it and gathering speed. I have mentioned what is happening in America, Australia, and the UAE, in China, India and Singapore, in Eastern Europe, East Africa and Indonesia. We are not the first movers in this global educational phenomenon of e-learning.

Within the UK itself, schools have begun to experiment with flipped classrooms, iPads for all, and blended learning. Schools are becoming equipped with wifi throughout the campus; they are decommissioning their PCs for virtualised desktops; they are replacing out-dated server rooms with Cloud servers. Teachers are demanding new technology because they read in the press that these learning tools are becoming available in other schools. Children have smartphones, and teachers realise that they are not just phones, but powerful computers linked to the internet by 3G. School leaders are realising that without the infrastructure to support hundreds of devices coming online every morning at 8:30am, the network will crash. This is very expensive, as well as very exciting. Governing bodies are investing many thousands of pounds every year on updated hardware, and as much again on software licences. Meanwhile, the expensive computer suite which is always good to show off to visitors on a tour is beginning to look tired. It is underused. Should it be decommissioned and returned to a good-sized classroom?

In 2012, as head of a different school, I wrote a piece for the HMC blog about the use of hand-held devices in the classroom. We had decided to implement a BYOD (Bring Your Own Device) initiative, and I was keen to take those to task who believed that allowing children to take devices into the classroom was dangerous, as these could be abused. I wrote:

> That is not a way to educate children. It is vital that we show the students how to effectively and practically utilise this powerful tool for good. Meanwhile we need to back this up with a system capable of supporting the effective use of such technology for learning in order that all our staff and students can bring their own devices to school to use wherever they are on site, and whenever there is an appropriate opportunity to do so. One of the key questions asked was whether the teaching staff would be sufficiently conversant with the technology to use it in lessons. The approach we advocate is simple: the children have the technology and know how to use it. The teacher knows what they want the students to discover. If the teacher works with the student, setting them interesting tasks in order to find out information or present findings, and also asks students to discover as many new ways as possible of deploying these devices, then the whole community will learn how best to make use of them. Our learning methods will be richly diverse, and bang up to date and adaptable to the new trends in technological innovation which come thick and fast, month by month. The first pupil to bring in the latest device will

be able to demonstrate new capabilities, making learning organic and engaging. The classroom will very quickly become a hive of activity. Our teachers and students will quickly become open to innovation. We will be prepared for the learning community and technological rollercoaster which exists in the world beyond school. So, mobile phones are no longer to be banned. Pupils may now bring in their own devices, and what we will expect is that they will be used in ways which are exciting, innovative and purposeful. Like any powerful tool, mobile technology itself is not dangerous unless it is in the hands of the inexperienced or malevolent. We are excited by the possibilities presented by opening our learners' minds to new methods and developing our staff alongside our pupils.

This was all stirring stuff at the time, and I was pretty proud of the fact that my senior leadership team and teachers were up for the challenge. However, there was a crucial missing element: strategy. I was pretty gung-ho about our BYOD. I saw it as an opportunity for low-cost staff development through an organic learning process in which pupils and teachers would learn together. In a recent email to the Deputy Head, Eddie Falshaw, at that school, I asked him to reflect, two years on, on any progress made since. He wrote:

> There seems to be an issue with the technology and that it will almost look after itself. Staff need training and showing how it can aid teaching and learning but more than that, if it is worthwhile it needs to be embedded into their practice and not seen as a one off/ flash in the pan.

> Furthermore, technology does not replace good teaching – teachers still have to teach and engage students in what they are learning. Failure to do this means that own devices are used for text and other 'off task' activities. This again sadly is a common feature. Teachers need to be vigilant and make it clear when it is appropriate or not to use the technology and be sure to engage their audience so that trying their mate's is the last thing on the child's mind!

> The trial and tribulations of misuse and inappropriate use are part of education - schools who ban devices are hiding, scared of the reality of the world today. By embracing technology and the issues surrounding it, we can empower all our students for the future.

In September, 2014, my current school is launching BYOD for its students. We have thought long and hard about the strategy, and have even postponed the launch by a year until we were sure that we had an appropriate infrastructure to carry the traffic which BYOD will divert through the school. An outline of the implementation strategy is as follows:

We identified four key decision-making stages for our BYOD strategy. First, it was important to seek to lay the foundations which would sustain future success with BYOD, obtaining supporters and ensuring that we had sufficient funding to undertake the first phase of readiness. Thereafter, the second phase involved planning. Thirdly, we are considering the implementation of the BYOD itself. In the future, we want to incorporate quality control methods in order to assess our progress, adjust and improve.

## Foundation strategy

Too many schools respond to a perceived need for a BYOD implementation because they feel that other schools are ahead of them, and that their children are missing out. However, to rush this is a mistake. A foundation strategy goes some way to ensuring that the complexity of a BYOD project is accounted for from the start.

First of all, we considered what BYOD would actually give to the school. We decided that BYOD would give us more skilled teachers and higher quality learning outcomes. As a school we believe in creative education which addresses every child's specific talents from our nursery students, through our Junior school, and into the Senior school. By focusing on these educational beliefs as a whole school goal we were able to demonstrate to those key decision makers that BYOD would allow us to personalise the learning of each individual student, while encouraging new, innovative and creative lessons from our teachers alongside their current repertoire of traditional classes.

In addition, the school believes in **Courage, Energy and Integrity**. BYOD epitomises a leap into the unknown, and pushing the boundaries (requiring courage), a commitment to a new way of working to develop exciting new forms of learning (energy), and trust that students and staff will learn to use their devices appropriately and sensibly (promoting integrity).

Aligning BYOD to the overall goals of the school helped us to be sure of the wisdom of the project, and to demonstrate its viability within our own school's context. Readers who have yet to implement BYOD in their own schools, or who are wondering how best to justify doing so to stakeholders, should think carefully about what matters most in their own school, and link this with BYOD. If the education of the children and teachers will be enhanced while upholding the values of the school, then it is a fit and a case can be made for supporting an investment of this kind.

At King's Ely, we had already developed a range of activities online via the school's VLE. Teachers were encouraged to use devices if they felt comfortable to do so in their lessons, and thus advocates and supporters were created through pilot projects. This also allowed us, before launching ahead, to weed out any potential difficulties or problems. A key one that we discovered was that we had an inadequate network set-up for the scale of the whole school project. As a result, we sensibly delayed the launch of BYOD and invested funds in developing a network which would not only sustain the programme, but also ensure its smooth implementation and sustainability as more devices came on stream. This cost money, but could be demonstrated to governors as a clear and present need. It also allowed us to scrutinise our whole school ICT infrastructure so that BYOD opened the doors not only to improvements in teaching and learning, but also the efficiency of our current structure and the skills and hardware needed to face the future, including cost savings which would be possible by operating within a leaner structure.

By setting up an ICT planning and curriculum group, we then were able to discuss and agree on project-specific goals for the implementation of BYOD and blended learning programmes which could fit with a whole school curriculum review due in 2014-15. These include a timeline, key milestones, budgets, staff professional development goals, infrastructure objectives and curriculum integration priorities. We also plan staff and pupil satisfaction surveys at regular points along the way. We took an inventory of all our hardware and tested the capabilities of the system to cope with increases in device traffic at key times, as well as speed of internet access at pinch points during the day. We aim to test the efficiency of our new network in order to ensure that it is indeed improving our service, coping with demand of users, reducing frustrations, and by this means can hold our service provider to account.

**Building support** is a key component of the foundation strategy, and a survey of teachers to establish their readiness to embrace change forms an important part of planning the BYOD part of our curriculum. This includes a check on what knowledge and experience colleagues already have of e-learning techniques, as well as assessing what training capability there is both in-house and from other training providers. The pilots which had preceded the launch, some of which had floundered due to connectivity issues are now encouraged once more with a reliable infrastructure. This serves the dual purpose of restoring faith in the school's investment in the wireless capability and also affirming the staff who had been willing to be guinea pigs first time around. They then became key advocates for their peers.

There are a number of suggested sources of support which the school needs to consider in order to mobilise the entire community. As well as the senior leadership team and governors, teachers, and even the teachers' union should be approached in order to demonstrate that such an initiative is in the interests of the staff as a whole. A focus on those early-established principles in line with the goals of the school should be maintained in any correspondence or public event.

SLT will be key in modelling the use of devices in meetings, and in their conversations with staff in many contexts. Governors can be included by enrolling them on an online course in order that they see the benefits and realities of online learning for themselves first hand and can discuss any misgivings or misunderstandings which they have with SLT. Teacher support can be gained by constantly feeding them examples of best practice, and by praising their own efforts. The magpie nature of the teacher, always on the look-out for a good lesson plan can be fed and nurtured through the Deputy Head (Academic) and the Heads of Departments. Union support can be gained partly through an approach which focuses on staff development and better working conditions. (I would suggest that a proactive approach from school leadership in such a way will be most welcome by unions, flattered that their support and advice is being sought by school leaders). Meanwhile the wider community, including children and parents, should be informed and excited by regular messages, question and answer sessions at parents' meetings, and 'have-a-go' days. All this will relentlessly feed the enthusiasm for, and develop the understanding of, what BYOD and blended learning actually are. After all:

> The hope of transforming schools through the actions of individual leaders is quickly fading ... An alternative conceptualisation is one where leadership is understood in terms of shared activities and multiple levels of responsibility (Alma Harris, 2008).

**Funding the programme** is a daunting prospect, and we certainly found that the various strands of ICT spending caused us some anguish as a SLT as we attempted to extricate ourselves from old ways of funding development while attempting to gain agreement to invest in new systems. A cost analysis needs to be clear and open to scrutiny. Tablets should cost less than PCs, and a BYOD strategy should put the cost of the tablet or smartphone in the hands of the parent. However, not all schools will be able to rely on family funding, and then there are the staff demands to be adequately resourced which a school must consider – one for discussion with the union, no doubt. There are a number of models, such as younger children learning through sharing devices, for example. However, a number of other strategies for making this more affordable include:

- Phasing projects over a couple of years. At King's Ely we brought in BYOD for our junior department first, but the planning meant that we do need to follow on the very next year as we receive children from our Junior School who expect the same standards. It was a commitment, but one we were able to budget for.
- Some online instruction materials are free, and as a result may generate savings if they replace textbooks. However, care has to be taken here as some licences are very expensive. Meanwhile, there

are some apps and programmes which are made freely available to schools.

- Professional development of staff can appear at first to be an enormous cost, although there are free online options for them as well (*eg* the Foundations of Virtual Instruction course from Coursera: www.coursera.org/virtualinstruction-002 ), plus the potential to use one's own staff as they become *au fait* with the technology.
- Reviewing the usage of software and hardware as the programme develops will lead to the discontinuation of unpopular or obsolete course materials, with resulting cost reduction.
- Seeking sponsorship is another possibility, depending on the context of the school.
- Grants may be available to schools seeking equipment, licences or training for staff
- Insurance schemes to cover repair and replacement costs.
- While this may be contentious, the increased delivery of online models, and the greater efficiency of network infrastructure may lead to a phased reduction of either teaching or support staff over time, especially in the case of support staff where there is an advantageous agreement with an external service provider working for the school on an out-sourced basis. A key person here is the network manager. He needs to know his onions, and should be regularly reviewed by an external consultant to ensure that advice being given to the school is sound.

All of the above gives the whole community confidence that the strategy has a strong plan behind it.

## Planning

In constructing the plan for implementation of blended learning a school should centre its approach around certain key areas:

- Our strategy and timeline
- Our school model
- Platform and content
- Devices
- Staffing and their development
- Improvement and measurement of impact.

**The timeline required** for a blended learning or BYOD phase should not be too short, as there needs to be scope for evaluation as well as implementation and embedding, but as things move relatively quickly in the education sector where technology is concerned, two to three years is long enough. This allows re-appraisal of budget commitments to ICT on a regular basis, while committing sufficient resources to make lasting changes beyond basic maintenance and short-sighted replacement of hardware.

The introduction of a new suite of GCSE and A-level specifications in the UK over the next three years from September 2014 also allows schools to consider their online strategy alongside major national curriculum and assessment changes. This is what we decided to do at King's Ely. Our BYOD capability was present by September 2014. Our Junior School was already experimenting with online learning and devices beforehand, and could announce BYOD at that time, but while our Senior School could do likewise, we are spending the autumn of 2014 considering the whole curriculum in order to take account of specification changes, our wider curriculum offering, and alongside this our planning for increasing blended learning and use of devices. This means that by September 2015 we should be in a good place to confidently roll out our first implementation phase, and this stage can be planned to last for two further years before changing, if necessary.

The year following September 2014 is an important planning year for the secondary education sector in the UK as the new examination specifications are announced, and political parties begin to posture in the run-up to an election the following spring. This means that it is an opportunity not only for individual schools to decide their strategy for blended learning, but for whole districts or sectors. With the macro-climate impacting upon all schools, the micro-climates of school or locality have opportunities to collaborate or go it alone and differentiate themselves. Yet again, this comes down to school leadership. Do leaders serve the school and its own ideals or the wider community (which of course may be a strategy to help all schools)? Different approaches to e-learning across schools can facilitate co-operation and creativity. High performing schools will need different things from this strategy than poorly performing schools. Private schools and maintained schools may offer differing experiences and this can either differentiate them from one another, or assist in a mixed economy which serves all children well.

An important strategy question is how to build in recognition of your lead teachers who may already be blending the learning or flipping their own classrooms. These advocates of the strategy, who are now pioneers of what you are hoping to achieve, need to be identified and championed, and where necessary rewarded and resourced. This may impact upon timelines, flexibility of a programme, professional development strategies or even budgets. An initial strategy is the use of a skills and tools audit, with an expectation of following up at points during the programme of implementation, or even delegating the task of the auditing process to one of the lead teachers who will be interested in discovering new tools and applications of e-learning. Planning the communication of this regularly through the school year is another important consideration.

Being clear about what we hope to learn from phases of the implementation, or from pilot studies is also important so that the focus remains on those priorities identified by the school leadership.

**The instructional model** that a school decides to implement should arise from discussion within the community, and not be imposed. The blended learning premise of boosting learning and developing staff through technology should be the key, and this requires integration of technology, not layering on top of the normal daily routine.

The discussion should consider different devices and also different online options in order that there is a full and frank appraisal of how these will genuinely benefit the pupils and teachers. Earlier I mentioned six potential blended learning models. These should all be discussed in order that the teachers can think about how their own professional practice might benefit from one model or another.

All this takes time and no small amount of work. However, the time invested now will make a real difference down the line and save the school from making some costly mistakes. It also ensures that all the staff can honestly say they were involved in the decision-making.

Meanwhile, the business needs of a school should be balanced carefully against the learning needs of the children. What needs to be considered is:

- Ratio of teachers to pupils (a key cost factor)
- Amount of autonomous online time per day (a key factor in reducing replication)
- Student performance

If these three needs can all be addressed in a way that maximises the results, this is a good thing. It pairs efficiency with strong student outcomes and the freeing of teacher time to deliver mentoring and tutorial support beyond their classroom activity.

Where sixth form students are concerned, there is a consideration of whether or not the Self Blend model is possible. This would lead to enhanced outcomes for students, but the school will need to plan the level of quality control that its teachers take responsibility for. The level of independence a sixth former is allowed to exercise will vary greatly between different school cultures, and perhaps even from student to student.

A key rule of thumb for all these blended learning possibilities is to ensure that the face to face elements improve the quality of human interaction, while the online aspects improve mastery, knowledge and skills.

At King's Ely we have a number of key decisions to make, based on the fact that, while we want to develop the level of core knowledge required of our students to perform in core subject examinations, we do not want to diminish the range of options which we offer our students, or the quantity and quality of the creative, artistic, musical and sporting activities which are on offer.

As a result, we need to decide whether the core and STEM subjects are taught with additional online content in order to protect curriculum time in other areas, or whether other elements of the curriculum are offered as electives with a large online component. Perhaps both are possible? Meanwhile, we need to decide whether we should ring-fence time for our extra-curricular activities, or create a more flexible offering which maximises the opportunity to use facilities during the school day, freeing up other times for timetabled lessons or online lab sessions. These are just some of the quandaries facing us, but with the possibilities available through e-learning, we have more opportunity to be flexible than might otherwise have been the case.

**Platform** choices will be an important feature of future development of BYOD, and it is better first of all to decide on learning goals and blended models, followed by an appropriate platform to support these, and then make choices about devices which support these platforms. There are a range of options, from a simple LMS (Learning Management System) which is built to support a range of course materials and is easy to monitor and manage, to a suite of tablet-based learning applications that are very difficult to manage. The range of options is constantly growing, and they include systems which offer learner profiling, assessment tools, instructional improvement systems, online learning providers, data platforms and tablet bundles. There are a range of providers, as outlined in the list below, and many more:

BrainHoney
e2020
Desire2Learn
Edmodo
Schoology
Buzz
Vschoolz
Apex
K12
Dreambox
i-Ready
Assistments
Wireless Generation
MasteryConnect
GooruLearning
PowerMyLearning

When choosing the platform, it is important that schools should integrate their school's Information Management System with their LMS so that there is a single sign-on for students and teachers. It is also important in view of the continually changing nature of the market that schools reject long-term contracts with platform providers or bespoke packages which may be expensive to extricate themselves from.

Some platforms do not support multiple content vendors, and these should be avoided, as should those which will not support content produced by the school's own teachers. It is also important that mark books and reporting functions can be supported by the platform which can then provide information on which teachers and pupils can act in order to create a competency-based learning environment.

**Content** options can be bewildering, as so much has been created in the past few years. As well as a shift from print media to digital, there has been a shift from flat digital content to adaptive and engaging software and applications. The content comes in a variety of forms: paid for content; open content and teacher-developed content.

Paid for content, usually purchased through a subscription, is often the more technologically advanced high quality content, which is why it carries such a premium. It often includes smart content which includes assignments and also carries gaming and feedback. There are also often quite sophisticated assessment packages within this content, and these packages are increasingly being bundled with these services as producers gain an understanding of what their customers require. A major UK provider is Pearson Education. Assessment is linked to the blended learning experience, and in much the same way as AfL is now commonly part of a face to face classroom environment, feedback and assessment are seen as key learning tools within a blended learning package. They are not just summative tests.

Open content is free content, available from a range of providers including universities, museums, the Khan Academy or the History Channel. There is a good deal of exciting content available from these providers for free, and as a consequence it is advisable to do research as a teacher or academic department before buying a paid for package wholesale, or demanding that teachers produce their own content.

Meanwhile, teacher content is growing in its sophistication and accessibility. Teaching their own online course allows the teacher to be more familiar with the online content when offering the support to students thereafter. Schools need to provide quality control of teacher-generated content, but there is also content which teachers are sharing with one another through sites like Edmodo, BetterLesson, TeachersPayTeachers, WeAreTeachers, and ShareMyLesson.

In any conversation with a provider of platform and content, the key question to ask is obviously, "How will your platform or content enhance the learning outcome for my students, or help my teachers deliver higher quality teaching?"

It is also advisable to find out whether course content is endorsed by examination boards, or indeed provides material which will be on a core specification.

Before a teacher films a lecture, it might be advisable to ask the questions:

- Why are they filming it?
- What are the students doing when watching the video lecture?
- Would the teacher be happy to watch the video?
- Why do the children need to understand and master the content within the lecture?
- What will the class follow-up activity be after they have watched the lecture, and how will this enhance the learning?

**Picking devices** is an area fraught with difficulty. On the one hand, a school wants children to be adaptable, while on the other it is good to develop skills which the teacher can be confident in assisting with. Tablets are cheaper, on the whole, than laptops, but there are some tasks such as extended writing which lends themselves more to a laptop than a tablet. Also, some tablets do not yet support the programmes or apps which a teacher might wish to use, so it is advisable to research the capability of a particular brand of device before a school embarks on a hefty mass purchase.

It is important, then to consider whether content you want will work on the device you are choosing. Potential costs are important, of course, as is the question of how much cost is transferred to parents (insurance charge, or the whole cost?).

Most schools now have acceptable use policies for ICT as standard now, but a refresh of the policy is advisable on a regular basis in order to protect schools, their staff and their pupils. These should go hand in hand with other policies on cyber bullying and security of possessions, for example, as well as behaviour and discipline policies.

**Differentiation of staffing** is a natural, although to some concerning, upshot of a blended learning strategy. In an ideal world, a school day which creates space for blended learning should also create space for teachers to spend more time on professional development, action research, collaboration with colleagues, and focused, meaningful face to face lessons with smaller groups of students, or even one to one mentoring. Mentoring is a powerful method of engaging pupils. It is advocated by Ken Robinson:

> Mentors open doors for us and get us involved directly in our journeys. They show us the next steps and encourage us to take them (*The Element*, 2009, p. 186)

In the USA, the schools which implemented blended learning also found that they were able to devise or consider a more differentiated ladder of staffing. This included master and apprentice teachers, instructors, coaches and lab specialists.

For example, KIPP Empower 'has developed a three-tiered staffing model with Lead teachers, Intervention Specialists and Instructional Assistants working together to give different types of instruction to small groups of children in a variety of settings' (Source: Educause).

One of the strengths of a differentiated team working with a group of students is not only that each pupil receives appropriate intervention in order to maximise their potential, but that staff also work in a high support environment and can learn specific skills from one another while developing their own area of expertise.

The main idea of teacher role specialisation is to focus excellent teachers' time on those instructional areas which are most critical for student success, or on high value non-instructional work which is related to student outcomes. This magnifies the effectiveness of the teacher. The teams of teachers have a team leader to whom all report, and who plans the interventions required for each individual child.

Other staffing models present in the USA include:

**Summit Public Schools:** A skill-based teacher development system with seven expertise areas identified: assessment, content, curriculum, instruction, knowing learners and learning needs, leadership and mentoring. Teachers are appraised against the seven areas, and placed on one of four levels: basic, proficient, highly proficient, and expert.

**Cornerstone Charter Health High School, Detroit:** There are no classrooms or year groups. Pods of 75 students work in a large open space. Teacher teams include individuals filling three different roles: Relevance Managers providing direct instruction and support to students in the design and evaluation of projects and internships; Rigour Managers oversee online coursework, provide support and set standards for mastery; Success Coaches work to help students make the transition to tertiary education and careers, providing practical advice as students consider life after school.

**Alpha Public School:** A middle school (GCSE equivalent) centring on self-contained classrooms where teachers deliver content in all core subjects. One Home teacher stays with a class of 34 students throughout the day and the year. During a lesson a Master teacher works with 17 of the students, engaging them through small group discussion and activities in one section of the room while the rest work on online content at individual computers, guided by their Home teacher.

**Touchstone:** Teachers have a career path that goes from Associate teacher to Master teacher. The Master teacher can earn up to $100k. Each Master teacher is responsible for all students in a core content area and responsibilities include teaching, but also training other teachers. All students have access to a Master teacher in each core curriculum area.

(Source: Educause)

These models are all specific to the context and culture of the individual school environment, and have evolved from a school considering what form of instruction fits it and its children best. In addition to differentiated and specialised jobs for teachers, blended schools also make use of 'distributed staffing'. These are usually part-time, or even at distance staff who deliver specialised content or act as peripatetic teachers. Paid as contractors, these could save the UK school in on-costs such as national insurance and pension.

There are clearly important considerations for a school thinking about a blended learning model. Not only would the cost of staffing be an important consideration, but also the management of disparate staff, new models of leadership, staff development programmes, and line management responsibilities. Each staff member would benefit from their own individual development plan (examples of these are available for access free of charge on www.bloomboard.com). In addition, these are such radical steps for a school to make that improvement and measurement of the impact of such models on pupil learning need consideration and planning. The joy of a wholly new system, of course, is that the performance management and data gathering process can be designed and implemented from the beginning, in consultation with staff. For a report on strategies for leveraging teacher talent with technology, Public Impact has outlined ten strategies. The report is available at www.OpportunityCulture.org.

## Implementation

The implementation of any major project is important to get right if it is to succeed, and by keeping in mind the main goals of a blended learning or BYOD strategy in school, leaders should keep the focus on teaching, learning and design rather than get sidetracked into hardware and software costs. The four areas to get right in the implementation of the strategy concern infrastructure, integration, professional development and ongoing support.

**Infrastructure** is a real potential barrier to success, and a lack of sufficient wifi coverage, broadband access, power, network equipment or facilities can be very frustrating when teachers are all ready to run with the technology. Upgrades to equipment cost a great deal of money, and take planning for the long-term (bear in mind that the long term in technology terms may only be ten years!). Essentially, if you have a two-lane A-road managing your current usage, and that occasionally snarls up in a blockage which the IT guys have to fix, God help you when BYOD starts and you need a ten-lane motorway to manage the increase in traffic. The system just will not cope. There are a host of companies which can provide advice and take a school's money, but try to find a company which specialise in schools and can work with you to find a range of options in planning the growth of your capability. Develop a relationship with this company, and you will make dramatic savings long-term. Check out your in-house IT staff. Many of them will be largely self-taught, and while they may be enthusiasts who serve the school well, they need to be absolutely technically aware if they are to cope with the sudden extra demands from all those new users wanting to do lots of exciting new things and assessments online.

Take steps to assess your current level of broadband access, and wifi capability, and gain an idea of how much blended learning you can support at present. For instance, maybe you can begin with sixth form, or just Key Stage 3. Plan the growth of this usage over the coming three years, and fix a roadmap of how you will extend the facility. Assess the potential for funding to deliver your plans. It may be that other schools or businesses are also needing to increase their broadband access. At a previous school of mine, we were fortunate enough to be situated across the road from a university. They already had excellent access, and we were able to capitalise on their proximity to the school.

It is also important not to underestimate the challenge of providing sufficient power to classrooms. If your school is looking at a laptop solution rather than BYOD this will be particularly significant as there will need to be space to charge machines. Older buildings may need a major rewiring upgrade to be safe. Is this really the correct solution for you?

Network management needs to be ongoing. It can be complex and costly – and more so if you have an inexperienced or poorly-skilled team. Could you out-source some of the network management, or use a company to update the skills of your current team? Are the team duplicating tasks? Do they keep information to themselves, or do they take time to train users on easily fixable functionality issues so that they do not become sidetracked by minutiae each day? Do they shop around effectively for new software and equipment, or do they have favoured suppliers? Challenge them about this.

Facilities will also need to be planned. Will there be as much need for larger teaching spaces? Will the school, in fact, require more large spaces for instruction? What upgrades within existing buildings will be necessary? Software is another potential money plughole. New app licenses, keyboards, antivirus software, headphones and webcams, laptop carts. The list is long, and has the potential to grow. There need to be important budget decisions made, tempered with potential savings, which may need to be demonstrated to governors.

**Integration of a school's information systems** is of the utmost importance if a school's blended learning initiative is to work efficiently. Teachers will need to generate class lists in a new application. Pupil assessments may need to be linked to the school's reporting system. Every user will require a single sign-on if time is not to be wasted in each new room or lesson.

**Professional development of staff** has been mentioned frequently in this section. It is not sufficient to simply demonstrate a new tool. What we are suggesting here is that teachers need to be prepared for deep changes in the very nature of teaching and learning. They will kick against this if they do not understand and agree with the path their school is taking. Professional development needs to focus on the benefits of differentiated teaching; classroom management, and the management of children working online; how to evaluate new resources, and help children to do likewise; how to instruct and assess in a blended learning environment. Some examples of training seminars could include:

- How to create engagement in the classroom.
- How to use new tools to enhance your teaching.
- Using real time data about progress to drive educational interventions in student learning
- How leaders can support teachers in a blended environment
- How to create and manage a blended school
- How to manage change
- How to communicate with stakeholders about the setting up of a blended learning environment
- How IT staff can set up a blended learning environment
- How IT staff can provide ongoing IT support for a blended learning system
- How IT staff can keep up with new technologies and innovation
- How network managers and teachers can work to procure appropriate equipment to support blended learning

**Technical support** for users with their devices is important, and this is where a plan concerning which devices the school intends to support is very important. Some manufacturers, such as Apple, are happy to do deals with a school in order to ensure that their own devices are used exclusively, and parents and students can be reassured that technical issues will be swiftly dealt with. Some support, of course, is online. There are schools who hire particular specialist support staff with the remit to fix glitches of this type. These tech coaches, who should focus on helping teachers and students to use technology and fix issues themselves where possible, should be separate from the technical support staff who fix the network issues when things go wrong. Each requires quite a different skill set. Some students have been deployed in technical support roles for classmates or younger students as a way of saving costs and also giving experience and responsibility to these students. They can also assist staff, of course. Children like to help and demonstrate their expertise in this way. A danger area is the fixing of a child's own device. The acceptable use policy should be clear that a school will not take responsibility for attempting to 'fix' a device bought by a child or parent, although advice may be given on where a child might get a device mended at the parents' expense.

**Implementation Support** is necessary because it will now be clear to readers that setting up a blended learning environment is a complex matter.

A project manager for the implementation process should be appointed either from within the school, or on a temporary consultancy basis from an external provider. The remit extends from supporting technology, instruction, staff development and communication. This is also an ongoing remit for an unspecified period as the school adapts to very far-reaching changes, and there may be further resources required to support the project manager. As the programme develops, the project manager should monitor how the needs of the school will shift from support to assessment of impact. The project manager's role as assessor grows naturally from the role as lead supporter of the implementation process.

**Communication is key** in any change management process, of course. Stakeholders will demand clarity about the implementation process, and messages should focus positively on the learning and teaching benefits of the blended system. Regular email updates about blended learning, and a monthly newsletter about online education and how the school is developing its resources and expertise will serve to reassure, and also to excite stakeholders. Building stakeholder confidence is of the utmost importance so that when glitches do occur they can be addressed as bumps in the road rather than catastrophes.

Communications should be particularly focused at times of the initial consideration of blended learning plans; the period of definition of the programme in the school's context; any key decision points; updates through the phases of implementation; and at measuring points, positively sharing the impact that has been made.

## Ensuring continuous improvement

Assessment of the implementation as it unfolds leads to an assurance of sustainability and progress. Key questions to ask on a periodic basis throughout the implementation phase are:

- Is this working, and how do we know? If not, why not?
- Can we improve this in any way?
- Are our teachers, parents and pupils pleased with what we are doing so far? What do they want to see next year?
- Can we demonstrate that more students are engaged in deeper learning? How will we demonstrate this comprehensively? When will we be able to be sure?

The assessment of available data needs to happen fairly frequently in order that the initiative does not drift, and so that interventions can be made if necessary. This requires a lot of work, and so should really be the main focus of the school for a short time period immediately following implementation.

Action research projects among teachers delivering blended learning lessons should be sponsored, and spread through the course of the implementation process. This will not only give valuable data, but also increase teacher advocacy and esteem regarding the process. Similarly, the inclusion of frontline teachers within the project management team as a troubleshooting working party can ensure ongoing assessment of the school-wide initiative.

The programme management group should be tasked with capturing lessons learned, documenting them, seeking solutions, and sharing its findings. Questions for this group might include:

- What has worked better than we expected?
- Where have challenges been encountered?
- Where have teachers been using technology well?
- Have we achieved cost savings in any areas? If not, what were the sources of expenditure which we did not predict?
- What can we do differently and better in the future?
- How can we document and disseminate lessons learned?

**Measuring the impact** will naturally take a certain amount of time due to the need to gather meaningful data about the impact on student learning and achievement. It is also important to differentiate between learning and achievement as concepts. While public examinations assess certain knowledge and skills, internal tests may have a different focus, depending upon the age of pupils and their point in education. It is vitally important to be realistic in the face of pressure from governors, parents and other stakeholders who may wish to see immediate impact.

It is advised to flag up and agree before the implementation process at what time reports on progress and measurements will be made. It is also important to agree when initial data should be taken. For instance, the novelty value of a new initiative may produce student and teacher engagement early on, which may then tail off. Initial findings may therefore be problematic. It may be better to hold off from making claims about data until the whole implementation phase has shown signs of settling. That is not to say that data shouldn't be taken, and assessments made. However, it is important to track the data over a significant time period.

**Future opportunities for innovative practice** should also be facilitated, due to the fact that technology is advancing all the time. Fostering future innovation, and creating opportunities for it will stop a school from making a big leap forward only to then stand still while other schools catch up and surpass it. The project management group should assist the assessment of future opportunities by asking what new problems have arisen that require a solution; what opportunities have occurred that should be taken; and how can we devise processes which will identify such problems and opportunities in the future?

Processes for innovation are also worthy of consideration. Who will take responsibility for being creative, testing innovative practice, and documenting the school's progress? What resources are necessary to do research in this area?

## What blended learning actually means

The above demonstrates that blended learning is not simply an initiative in trying to use new technology in the classroom. It is actually about changing the culture of the learning environment as it currently is. This is what is so hard, and why movement on this appears to be so slow in the UK. Nobody wants to be first to commit to something which is so radical, and so there are many piecemeal attempts at integration which, with some moderate successes, are beginning to change attitudes to teaching and learning in small pockets of the UK schools system. However, in view of the developments seen in other parts of the world, where current education provision is either not accessible to all, or is seriously flawed, there have been some real advances. These are parts of the world which need to develop new environments. Perhaps in the UK we do not need to ... at least not yet. However, what our children will need is to take their place in a world in which other children have had the advantage of developing independent learning, adaptability, resourcefulness, academic rigour and a world view. Blended learning is helping them to do so. Their teachers are also becoming better and better at developing online content, utilising current online models, and facilitating individualised learning. This means that before too long, UK teachers may be seen as old-fashioned and set in their ways, and the other parts of the English speaking world will be seen as more able to deliver a modern education in the lingua franca of English: North America, Canada, Australia, and South Africa, perhaps?

The methodology for bringing about a blended learning culture shift in a school is set out above, and comes after tried and tested initiatives in the USA have demonstrated how to go about it. It is possible with clarity of thought, focus and hard work. There are obstacles to be overcome, but the alternative does not bear thinking about: the UK education system falling behind the rest of the world because it failed to move quickly enough. There is certainly one sector of UK education which really should be sitting up and taking note: the independent fee-paying sector. Now unaffordable for the vast majority of UK families, the very clientele which have given it its USP are deserting, in spite of the fact that they would love to stay. There are fewer first-time UK buyers than ever before, put off by the cost. Not that these folk believe independent schools are not worth the money. They simply cannot afford to stretch that far, and they will not usually give one child the chance of independent school at the expense of their siblings. So, as a result, a generation is being lost to independent education. It means that good schools will either perish or look to enter the maintained sector

– losing their independence. Otherwise they will rely on a niche market or an overseas boarding community of the super-rich. These will not remain, however, if the standards of education they see in the UK begin to fall behind those of other countries. They will take up places in more forward-thinking schools overseas.

The UK independent sector only educates just over 7% of UK children, so why is this relevant to UK education as a whole? More fool them if they have priced themselves out of the market at a time when investment in the maintained sector allowed advancements which made a real difference.

Well, actually the diminishing of our independent schools has an impact on UK education as a whole. The brand of Eton, Cheltenham Ladies College and Rugby is our quality assurance mark overseas. It attracts students not only to our boarding schools, but also to our universities and maintained sector boarding schools and sixth form colleges. Independent schools may well only educate 7% of our children, but still account for 25% of our university students, and almost 50% of the intake of Oxbridge – not because of prejudice and the old school tie network, but because of expertise in preparing children for examinations and university entrance, and the aspirational culture which pervades in these schools.

'Classroom in the Cloud' may still seem a pipe dream, and too difficult to achieve, but with a will to make it work there is no reason why UK schools should not seize the advantage while there is still the opportunity to do so.

# Chapter 6

# Seizing our opportunity. Options for UK schools

**Some see things as they are and ask why. I dream of things that never were and ask why not?**

George Bernard Shaw, Back to Methuselah, 1949

THROUGHOUT THE book so far I have attempted to demonstrate the ways in which education is changing worldwide, and yet that Britain is in many ways failing to move quickly. This may be because we are confident in our current offering, or it may be because we are relatively unaware of the ways in which online learning is developing for school age children around the globe.

I have also made the point that mistakes have been made by those who have rushed in to online learning without fully considering the ways in which teaching and learning might benefit from the changes. As a result, there have been some expensive errors, and faltering initiatives. This gives credence to the view that we should retain our cautious and gradual movement towards online learning, confident in the strengths of what we know we currently deliver.

We have considered the benefits, but also some of the drawbacks of online learning, and this has led us to a view that the teacher must be retained as a vital feature in an educational system of the future.

I have outlined an approach to planning a blended learning curriculum in a school, and demonstrated that it is possible, with the right leadership, will and focus on learning and teaching objectives which fit in with the values of a school. The difficulty comes in cultural shift and stakeholder belief. These are not insurmountable obstacles to change, but they are significant, most notably in view of the incumbent's dilemma, and the factors which embed caution or denial where potentially disruptive change is concerned.

In this chapter, I will seek to make the case for the fact that the time for us to grasp the nettle over online learning is now upon us. The timing is critical because we need to maintain our competitive advantage worldwide, while delivering the most relevant and engaging curriculum we can for our students. I will also make the case that UK schools can not only make these changes, but can in fact become world leaders in the provision of this type of education if we act now. Otherwise we will miss our chance, and our future will become uncertain. A key part of this chapter will be focused on our independent schools – my own area of expertise – and how we can address a major crisis which currently stares us in the face while retaining our world class quality mark. It may be that maintained sector schools can exercise elements of independence in their leadership in order that their students can benefit in a similar way, or even collaborate with their independent neighbours in order to raise the standards of UK education to new heights for all our children.

## The Innovator's Dilemma

In their book, *Disrupting Class: How Disruptive Innovation Will Change The Way The World Learns* (2008), Clayton Christensen and his co-authors Horn and Johnson make the point that by 2019 more than half of high school students in the USA will be learning online. This may be America's tipping point for online learning or it may already have been reached. America is – for all its similarities – culturally, economically and politically different from the UK. However, the various drivers for the country moving towards online learning are very similar. The USA was enduring bleak budgets for its public schools. It faced teacher shortages in core subject areas. There was pressure to expand the curriculum, improve outcomes, and to reduce drop-out rates. Meanwhile there was a growing commercial market in virtual schooling within the tertiary sector which meant that online learning was becoming more and more accessible to undergraduate students. Politicians could see the potential for cost savings, and entrepreneurs could see niche markets ripe to be served by virtual learning. As early as 1976, John Sperling, a Cambridge-educated economist, founded the university of Phoenix as a for-profit university for working adults with distance learning packages. Later Keith Oelrich, CEO of Insight Schools, founded an online virtual school to address the problem of teenage dropouts from education. It now runs 120 courses and has 24/7 assistance for students. Ron Packard, the CEO of K12inc, founded a virtual school in order to create a level playing of access to education for those who could not previously afford school. His company provides 1:1 tutoring and monthly face to face meetings with the online tutor as well as a suite of top quality courses. Barbara Dreyer founded Connections Academy which, as well as online courses, also engaged teachers to write virtual textbooks and other electronic resources. Julie Young founded the Florida Virtual School, which now has thousands of students with all sorts of profiles, and which is a school Florida students have the right to choose, while funding is obtained by charging students who wish to be educated through its network from outside the state of Florida itself.

All these conditions exist in the UK now. What is less developed is the online schools market. (A word of caution, the term 'virtual school' has a particular UK context. It is a concept which is applied to an over-arching care system for looked-after children. While they attend normal school, they benefit from a local authority 'virtual Head teacher' who ensures that the children in this category within the locality have the full services they need in school, and offer support beyond. So, it is not blended or online learning).

Meanwhile there have been some first movers in the UK market offering online services, usually for a fee:

- Academus offers education services for school age children, CPD and online tuition for healthcare professionals.
- InterHigh Education (www.interhigh.co.uk ), which opened way back in 2005, charges fees for virtual schooling, as 'an independent school on the internet', but is a not for profit organisation. Lessons are delivered wholly online through synchronous learning. The pupils come from all over the world. Their lessons are archived in a lesson library which allows asynchronous learning as well. It says that it is flexible, positive, quality and accessible. Inter High Advanced is an A-level programme currently charging £840 per subject per year. A four subject A-level course fee of £3360 is certainly more affordable for parents than fees of a traditional independent school. Fees 2013-14 for a student between Years 7-11 were £2280.
- On July 1, 2012 the *Sunday Times* reported that one of the new free schools to be signed off by Michael Gove the Secretary of State for Education would be the first local authority online school in the UK.
- On September 28, 2006 BBC News reported 'Virtual School beats the real thing' in a report about First College (an online school opened in January, 2006).

- A brief Google search also revealed Briteschool (the British e-school); The Virtual School, (www.thevirtualschool.com) with a mission to pass the best teaching available to children worldwide for free; Periplus Education (www.peripluseducation.com) for schools who are thinking of outsourcing some of their education provision; Virtual College, which offers a secondary curriculum delivered by qualified teachers live online as a 'drop-in E-cademy'; and then there was Net School (www.net-school.co.uk) 'an English education online', founded by Susan Reed in 2009, with individual tuition at £30-35 per hour plus 20% VAT. Also £180 + VAT a term per two hours of each GCSE subject tuition per week.

Most of these schools appear to have small numbers of students, many of whom have had a poor experience of mainstream school in one way or another. The confidence-building and strong pastoral focus of these schools was tangible in their marketing material, which either says something about the children who currently make use of the service, or about the barriers they face in convincing parents that a wholly online school is really up to the job of caring. This may also be something to do with the fact that these schools seem to be almost entirely online in nature, rather than blended offerings. This cuts down considerably on overheads (Nisai school in Stockton-on-Tees has one computer room full of soundproofed booths at which teachers sat at computers delivering lessons). However, the synchronous nature of most of these schools' lessons meant that teachers did have to be there and engaged with pupils in real time. This actually has benefits of helping a relationship to develop between teacher and learner. They are, after all, interacting with one another (although the teacher would not be able to pick up the visual clues which they might have in a face to face context) through mail and social networking, managed by the school. Parents login, too, so that the teacher might spend some time interacting with them. On the other hand, there is a limit to the size of class that such a teacher can teach because of the need for them to be responsive to pupil comments within the lesson itself.

One of these online schools celebrated its students as 'a new generation of learners who can take full advantage of their leading edge'. This may well be the case for some, and it is certainly the goal in a best case scenario. I did find that something was missing here: the in-school experience. These were online schools, and not blended schools, as far as I could tell. There is therefore still space in the market for an established traditional school, or group of schools, to develop a blended offering.

## First movers
Earlier I discussed the incumbent's dilemma when we considered the problem for a successful school in engaging with disruptive technology, and

even acknowledging it in the first place. However, let us say that a Head, or even a senior leadership team or board of governors in a school decides that, yes, there is a case for changing. Things are not magically likely to fall into place. There becomes a new dilemma facing the school which might want to be the first mover: the innovator's dilemma.

I have mentioned Clayton M. Christensen before with regard to his book, *Disrupting Class* in which he prophesied that education would change due to disruptive technologies. In a previous title, *The Innovator's Dilemma. When new technologies cause great firms to fail* (1997, 2000), he explains why 'sound decisions by great managers can lead firms to failure'. This is echoed by Jeffrey Pfeffer in his gem of a book, *What Were They Thinking? Unconventional wisdom about management* (2007):

> Relatively few companies actually embrace the management practices that are required to help them get smarter. That's because some of the things they need to do to learn are counterintuitive.

Christensen seeks to resolve the problem, prescribing managerial solutions and saying that leaders should seek to harness the principles of disruptive innovation. I have tried to address these principles (below in bold), adapting his findings about diverse industries, and applying them to education.

**Principle 1: Companies depend on customers and investors for resources.** While managers and leaders *think* that they control the flow of resources, they in fact do not. This is because without listening to customers and delivering, the business won't gain resources. It will not survive unless it satisfies the customer. As a result, the best companies have very well developed processes for killing ideas that customers do not want, and as a result they find it very hard to invest sufficient time and resources in disruptive technologies.

Good Headteachers and their Deputy Heads know that parents want strong teachers with excellent classroom skills and good knowledge and discipline. They want the school to be well resourced. They want a school to have good facilities. They want their children to perform well in examinations. Our customers are the parents, and they are becoming more discerning, in both the independent and the maintained sectors. In the independent sector, the customer drives all that a school can do, as these tend to be not for profit schools, with fee income the main, if not the only, source of income. Certainly it is the case that senior managers in schools are beginning to develop customer service, and give parents a large amount of time to consult over changes or to discuss issues directly relevant to their children. Our systems in schools are set up to please parents and children to an increasing degree, and so are therefore attuned to killing the ideas our customers (parents) don't want, and making ourselves leaner and more focused as a consequence. There are a number of reasons for this, from the focus on seeking to provide a bespoke package for each child, to an understanding that with increasing choice, parents could move elsewhere, with the resulting downturn in income for the school. Numbers on roll matter enormously. In addition, there is the increased likelihood of litigation in our present environment, meaning that schools spend increasing amounts of time and money on seeking legal advice or writing and amending policies. Nobody wants to make a costly mistake, and increasingly schools are understanding the business principles of customer service. Parents are also important stakeholders with whom to engage if changes are proposed. They are emotionally attached to the school because they have chosen to send their children to the school, and want to feel that they have made the correct decision. If changes are likely to affect their children, they need to be convinced, and frankly there are those who do not care a great deal about the long-term future of the school. What matters to them is the here and now and the service that they and their children currently receive. As a consequence of all this, we must take care, because why invest in new things our customers do not want? How can we convince current parents that they may like the future change if we have not the evidence to demonstrate the benefits?

This is where strong, independent leadership is so important in our schools. By independent leadership, I am not only talking about the independent sector. The recent changes in the level of autonomy in school leadership is one of the most exciting developments in the maintained sector in the UK over the past decade and a half. Free from the dead hand of the LEA, the academy or free school Head and governors are able to make decisions which may be radical and unilateral. It is an exciting time, but depends on strength and clarity of purpose. Rather than the default position that customers drive the business as managers seek to please, there needs instead to be firm and unequivocal articulation of mission by school leadership, and the strength of character to be prepared for some current parents to leave, as they will be unconvinced. It is something of a gamble.

Perhaps the answer is that we build, alongside our current school offering, a new and autonomous business based solely around the disruptive technology? This can then be killed off if unsuccessful, but integrated if successful.

**Principle 2: Small markets don't solve the growth needs of large companies.** Disruptive technologies enable new markets to emerge. In terms of education, without online or blended learning, there would be no online learners. The very existence of the capability to deliver online lessons creates a new market which had never been there before. However, the market has begun small because as yet the full potential of an online educational offering has not been fully realised. It challenges our perceptions of 'good' education, and we need to be convinced. While the market remains small, it is unlikely to be taken seriously by schools who depend on large numbers of pupils.

Not all of our schools need to grow, but those which depend on fee income certainly need increasing numbers of pupils in order to maintain a broad curriculum offering, well-rewarded, quality teachers, and well-maintained and developing facilities. Following recession, many independent schools have found that their usual customer base has begun to desert them, and as a consequence they must either win these back, or look to a new market. Boarding schools have done this by seeking out markets for overseas boarders. The British boarders are a dwindling group, and overseas students have ensured the survival of some boarding schools. Boarding schools have also expanded their populations of day students in order to maintain their expensive boarding model. However, boarding schools now find themselves needing to consider more options. Do they offer weekly or flexi-boarding? How far do they expand the day offering? How can they differentiate fees in order that day students can afford what is on offer? Meanwhile day schools have no boarding market to tap into, so how do they increase their range of students? Do they look to running new transport offerings in order to access children from other geographic areas? Do they reduce fees to make their schools more affordable? In maintained schools, can they expand facilities in order to grow the school and take on new catchment areas? Can a group of parents set up a free school in an area that they do not feel is well served by current provision? There are a whole host of problems and challenges for schools, but with a bricks and mortar facility, geography, politics and money are the key factors, and there is a limit to the level of expansion possible. Significant advantage is to be gained over competitors by companies entering emerging markets first, the evidence tells us. Understanding the size of the market, however, is what makes sense to most managers. How does a manager within a business assess the size of a market which is not yet there? Profits and customer base need to be linked to cost. An independent school with a fee income of £15million wishing to grow by 10% per annum needs £1.5million more next year. In terms of numbers on roll for my current school, this would equate to as many as 100 more students. The current market may not be large enough, and as a result new markets need to be explored.

A smaller business with £1million turnover obviously needs just £100,000 of new sales for the same level of growth. As a consequence, new entrants or smaller players can seek out new markets as they have less to lose by making mistakes, and more modest requirements for growth.

For the larger schools, it is not possible to wait until the new market is large enough to be interesting, because we will not have invested in the new technology. As a result we will not be able to catch up, and will lose any opportunity to enter this market. Smaller organisations can respond more easily to the opportunities for growth in the emerging market. We need to fully explore the emerging market. The only way to do so is to leap in and begin offering some alternative models to groups of parents. This is where many schools will worry. Will current stakeholders get twitchy? Will their own children benefit from new models, or will these be aimed at new entrants or distance learners? Will a school develop online lessons as a new income stream, or as an integrated part of their package for current pupils? All in all, these decisions need making by the leadership. They need to be firm decisions, because, yet again, they fly in the face of conventional wisdom concerning the running of the school as a business.

**Principle 3: Markets that don't exist can't be analysed**. Excellent managers carry out good quality market research, upon which they base a well thought through plan, and then execute the plan. The planning is based on reason and feasibility, as well as what is *known*. Because most innovations are sustaining in character, most managers have learnt to manage in a sustaining context, such as market trend analysis, measuring customer satisfaction, and planning a well thought out response. With disruptive technology this isn't possible. There is little known about the emerging market and the ways the new technology will serve customers in that market. As a result, first movers get maximum advantage. But there is a dilemma for the innovator- without firm predictions and knowledge, innovators must plan for the fact that predictions and their strategies may be inaccurate.

This may terrify the governing bodies and leadership teams of many schools. Their natural conservatism – especially as governors, and so trustees of a school – will be crying out for a cautious approach to such radical approaches to forward planning. But this "discovery-based planning" stops the paralysis or wrong decisions which come from seeking certainty in a changing environment. It can even assume that forecasts are wrong. This drives a development of knowing only what needs to be known, and this is very effective. It also leads to calculated risks based on an unfolding expertise. This development of expertise through the planning process leads to a more nimble approach to the planning process, and a more efficient one. Schools who choose such an approach to their planning of a response to emerging, disruptive technologies will learn more about the market, develop confidence in decision-making, and understand more about their own capabilities in dealing with risk. This will translate to other parts of the school, and lead to genuine dynamism. Yet again, however, the point to stress is that this needs strong and clear leadership in order to establish focus, maintain focus, and impose necessary controls. It also requires, and develops, two other important elements of leadership in schools; a willingness to take responsibility, and to trust in one another as a team of leaders.

**Principle 4: An organisation's capabilities define its disabilities.**
Usually we would decide on a strategy and assign a group of employees we

feel are capable to the task, assuming that we will be successful as they have been proven to be adaptable and have certain skills. But with disruptive factors, the flexibility and trainability of employees to the new ways of thinking are one thing. The capability to adapt procedures and values is quite another.

Pfeffer suggests that what is necessary is an ability to let employees try out innovations and fail:

> failing early and failing often is better than failing once, failing at the end, and failing big. The principle is simple – learn and fail on a small scale. But that ethos requires accepting that novelty and innovation are invariably accompanied by setbacks and failures. And embracing such a way of operating requires letting people fail – maybe even encouraging them to fail. (p. 37)

Processes and values designed for the old way of doing things may not be fit for purpose for the new technology. Values lead to prioritisation, and with disruptive technologies these may work against what was formerly held to be valuable to the school, and so will not be prioritised. Leaders in schools need tools to create new capabilities in the face of disruption. I have heard teachers and leaders in schools say that they encourage children to stumble and fail, because that is how they learn, and yet in reality children are hammered with detentions for failing. They are driven towards success, and teachers are also slapped hard for getting things wrong. Schools often pay lip service to the concept of learning through trial and error. We should embrace it.

First, look at the resources required to succeed. Do we have them? Then look at the processes and values we have to succeed. Can we change the processes and adapt the values? Do we want to? This is a fundamental question which the leadership of the school needs to ask before embarking on any far-reaching changes. It is also important that the discussion about the values of the school is multi-layered, because people within the school need an opportunity to explore and fully understand what the school stands for, and the implications of adapting to a blended learning model. What may at first seem to be counter to the school's values might actually embrace them. Can the school embrace failure? What a question to ask!

My own school is a boarding community which has a mission to find the very best in each child, and to develop that specialism within the context of a broad and balanced curriculum. The school also believes in developing 'Courage, Energy and Integrity' in our pupils.

On the one hand a blended learning model may allow students to be focused on developing their skills, and travelling at their own pace through a course. It may serve exactly the value of developing a child's individual talents. However, as a community there may be some stakeholders who feel that there is something too individualistic about all of this, and that children sitting in their own rooms following an online course actually diminishes something very valuable about the school: namely community. It is an interesting starting point for a discussion, and of course, the form of words with which one addresses the impact of blended learning on a school will need to be agreed. Such a discussion can also lead to a clear definition of blended learning within our own context. For instance, the tutoring which goes alongside the blended learning model becomes fundamental, and having tutors attached to the houses which are the bases for children throughout the day becomes even more fundamental in order that we have pastoral care linked to the community structures which support children beyond the classroom. Such a discussion opens the minds of those charged with implementing the new technologies, and develops the capacity and capability of these staff while overcoming preconceived ideas: the disabilities which might have hamstrung a school previously.

If a school community is unable to get past the fact that this fundamental change to the way education is delivered is deeply concerning, then perhaps the school needs to consider whether blended learning is integrated within the old structure of schooling, or whether perhaps the answer is to form a new venture in parallel which incorporates the new processes and values? One of the key values to inculcate is one of embracing change and seeking solutions.

**Principle 5: Technology supply may not equal market demand.** In the beginning, the disruptive technologies within education which have created capabilities for online learning have existed on the periphery of the mainstream, serving small markets such as sick children learning from home, or school refusers who cannot face coming in to school day after day. However, what makes them disruptive to our current model of school is that these small enterprises which use the technology – online schools – then develop techniques, applications and products which respond to the needs and values of their growing market. As they develop, such applications can – and indeed have – become fully competitive within the mainstream market against the established order. When the performance of one product has evolved to beyond what the market demands, and the inferior product has evolved sufficiently to meet the market demands, the competitive factor left is PRICE.

This is where the independent sector in UK education now finds itself. The basis of product choice for the consumer naturally evolves from functionality, to reliability, to convenience, and then to price. In our efforts to stay ahead by developing a competitively superior product, independent schools in the UK have unwittingly moved too far up-market too quickly. We have produced schools which are far more functional than those with fewer opportunities and facilities. Look at the facilities arms race;

curriculum innovation; and personalised, bespoke learning experiences that we have been delivering. We seek to be ever reliable, but in an age of email communication 24/7 we have become more accountable and more open to parental scrutiny, and have to work extraordinarily hard to remain reliable. We have tried to become more convenient for working parents, as have all our competitors, so parents now have far more choice available as schools have restructured their working days, offered more clubs, and put on more transport links in order to make it as easy as possible for children to attend. It all costs money. Our fees have risen to accommodate all this excellent customer service, and to attempt to stay ahead of all our competition in both the independent and maintained sectors. As a result, we have become unaffordable for the majority of parents.

On top of that, independent schools are being more heavily scrutinised by the more demanding and financially squeezed consumer; a natural consequence when they are paying prices which are rising above the rate of inflation. When there is no alternative, this may be something which a business need not worry too much about (although there are clearly ethical considerations, of course). For UK independent schools, this is no longer the case. There are excellent maintained sector providers with facilities, curriculum options and teaching expertise which is comparable to the independent sector in many areas of the country. Overseas, there are an increasing number of international schools and British curriculum schools being set up, offering lower cost education by English-speaking teachers on the doorsteps of families who may find it hard to send their children overseas to school, or who may not be able to do so. As the reputations of such schools grow, UK schools will need to justify their fees. I believe that they are value for money, and they are usually very well stewarded by governors and leaders. However, the problem is price. We have provided a vacuum at lower price points which competitors with disruptive products can enter. We need to look carefully at how our customers access and use education in order to discern when might be the appropriate point to adapt or reject current teaching and learning models in favour of improved or even totally new ones.

We have three questions to answer. First, how can we defend ourselves against new entrants to market; disruptive attacks, such as lower-priced models which offer bespoke online learning packages for those with less money to spend; and alternative models which may be more flexible, and offer a disruption-free learning environment, or learning at any time or place? Second, can we identify potential disruptive technologies or products around which our school or market can be built? Third, how do we take the disruptive technology seriously without putting at risk the relationship with our most loyal or most profitable customers?

The problem for UK independent education in fact is that many of our schools have decided to invest heavily in what we believe the market wants, and in doing so have tried to be all things to all people. This has been a failure in understanding the independent school market place appropriately. Our best schools have tried to sustain themselves and their model in every conceivable way at a time when the market is shifting, becoming discerning, and has been impacted upon by the internet in many other aspects of life. As a consequence, we have failed to differentiate ourselves by market segment and instead have spent too broadly, driving up our own costs. We are not alone in this, but are behind the curve somewhat. Our parents, all working in industries which have had their own issues with dealing with disruptive technology are either frustrated and bemused by our lack of adjustment, or are themselves blind to the fact that education is a business, and seek reassurance in the comforting traditionalism of what we stand for and deliver. The problem with the former group is that they soon become so frustrated that they lose faith in us and seek more forward-thinking alternatives. The problem with the latter group is that they hold us back from innovation, and diminish our capacity for creativity. In the words of Christensen: "It is as if leading firms are held captive by their customers."

The internet is the infrastructural technology which enables the disruption of very many industries. It is an innovation affecting everybody, and as such brings new values and possibilities into play when an industry is deciding next steps. Some of these values and possibilities build upon former ways of doing things, and as such are sustaining innovations, rather than disruptive ones. Our managerial decision-making, and also the expectations of our customers, can make simple sense of these innovations and they can even affirm the need to change or develop. For instance, the availability of YouTube on the internet allowed teachers to show clips to supplement their teaching, and allowed children to create presentations to classmates in a novel way. This created an extra tool for teaching and learning which enhanced the current offering, and could be demonstrated in the mainstream classroom with the use of an interactive whiteboard. Schools could justify spending many thousands of pounds on the interactive whiteboards as tools to enhance the learning experience, and can justify this as a sustaining innovation.

However, the ability of the internet to deliver whole courses online disrupts the usual model of school. As a consequence, a school leadership finds it difficult to wholly embrace it because leaders within a school will seek to protect the school against the unknown. In a sense, they are building protective walls around their community. This is a task of leadership: to protect.

In other industries we often see that innovative products were developed within industries by those below the level of senior leadership. Often the technologies would go through several versions before being pitched to senior managers. We saw this with the first digital camera being developed by a Kodak engineer, but as this threatened Kodak's main business of film it was not embraced by the firm. Similar innovations occurred, according to Christensen, at Seagate Technology and Memorex in the disk drive industry.

In such industries, the idea, pitched to leadership and receiving a lukewarm reception, can often lead to developers taking their innovations elsewhere. It is then interesting to see established firms attempts in these industries to cope with the disruption. Christensen takes us through several key steps:

1. Disruptive technologies were first developed within established firms.
2. Marketing personnel then sought reactions from their lead customers, who could not see how their current requirements would be served by the new technology.
3. These confirmed in the minds of leaders in established firms that sustaining technologies should be developed.
4. Innovators formed new companies to sell their innovations, and found and developed the new markets which were not being served by the established firms.
5. The new industries then began to move more up-market by adopting sustaining improvements to their products and developing these products, exploiting the large market gains possible while incorporating aspects of the markets ahead of them for the client gap who were looking for a more affordable alternative than the established firms.
6. Established firms then belatedly jumped on the bandwagon to defend their customer base. By this time the new technology had become fully performance competitive with the established firms. Price became the key, but the disruptive character had now gone, meaning that established firms were being undercut by a quality product with which they could not compete as they had little understanding or expertise to draw on within the new area.

There is a lesson here to leadership to think ahead when confronted with innovation, and not to follow customers, but to form customer opinion through strong leadership and marketing. In schools, providing a strong leadership voice with an educational narrative allows the marketing of new educational methods to take hold. This is the basis in my belief that we can act now to take the lead in this area before we are disrupted. We do not want to jump on the bandwagon belatedly once the early adopting online schools develop the pastoral care and extra-curricular opportunities which can see them move from wholly online communities to establishing tutorial centres for their online students to gain face to face access, but need to do so now and seize the reins so that we can access the wider market which may be available for us.

Incumbents often listen to their most profitable customers, rather than the market as a whole. As a result, they tend to marginalise themselves and lose market share. An independent school in the UK needs to take a decision on whether it becomes one of the dwindling number offering an exclusive and luxury product, or to aim for a more 'mid-market' position. In partnership with state schools, an independent school can extend its reach to new markets, extend the range of public benefit, and increase its own subject portfolio for current customers.

This means that we need to listen to those who may leave us, or not look at us in the first place. We also need to consider what new products we can offer to diversify our customer base.

There have been various programmes offered already which we can learn from in other countries:

In Florida alone, 220,000 children are being educated in state-funded virtual schools. There has been significant recent enrolment growth, especially among children excluded from mainstream schooling, or unable to access it because of illness and disability.

In addition, there are multi-district online schools. These are full-time schools which affiliate to fund an online programme from which they all share resources. This is funded through a mixture of public funds, grants and fees paid for courses which the consortium sells to other schools and districts.

Consortium programmes are hybrid programmes which are developed and run by a major education provider. Online content is controlled and distributed through the consortium's network of schools nationally and internationally.

Finally, there are post-secondary programmes. These are recovery courses made available for students who have under-performed, and wish to re-sit; or indeed for adult learners who may have left school some time ago without qualifications, and seek to enhance their employment prospects.

An independent school must consider its relationship with maintained sector providers. There are opportunities available for the independent to increase its public benefit, and for maintained sector students to learn from teachers in the independent in ways which may not be available in their own school. This cuts both ways of course. In order to diversify the curriculum offering and opportunity in the independent school, its students can use resources and access courses and teaching from the academy in the same way. The blurring of lines between paying for education or collaborating for free will need to be discussed as a philosophical and ideological issue between the schools, but also needs to be considered by parents of both establishments. In some regions I can see there being some excellent initiatives being developed by school partnerships of this type, but not in all regions by any means.

In addition, independent schools may club together in a consortium in order to share teaching and resources, but in other circumstances may find themselves in direct competition with one another, which will inhibit co-operation.

The four factors to bear in mind with investment in disruptive technologies are:

- They are simpler and cheaper than our traditional classroom-based approach to teaching, so we need to assess the outcomes carefully over time. As we are two years or so behind the USA, UAE and various other countries we have data from these which we can begin to draw upon. Nevertheless we must apply our own cultural conditions to any research.
- Blended learning models may well cost less to produce and run than the traditional face to face approach. However, the maintenance costs and quality control aspects need to be factored in, not to mention the network and licensing requirements of a blended model. The difference in income comes through having an entrepreneurial approach to developing wider markets.
- They are first commercialised in markets which are emerging, or appear to be insignificant to the incumbent business. We must overcome the incumbent's dilemma and seek to be innovators.
- The most profitable customers don't want new innovative models, (initially at least). They have already bought the traditional approach. It is those customers who did not choose us or even look at us that we need to pursue. So the least profitable customers are likely to embrace the innovation initially. This appears counter-intuitive to the incumbent. Why go after new customers who will yield lower profits? Blended learning, rather than wholly online courses, gives us opportunities to expand our offering into new markets, while our new position as a first entrant then allows us to adapt the new technology in sustaining ways to attract the best of the most profitable customers when they eventually become advocates of the technology and it has lost its 'disruptive' characteristic.

The gamble is actually on the faith that the innovation is likely to genuinely revolutionise the market and the current product range available. Will the profitable customers shift? Will the flight to quality which the independent schools have long been reassuring themselves about actually become a flight to affordability, which tends to suggest that quality will be sought after sufficient people switch to the affordable? What I hope we will see is quality made more affordable. If the independent sector can pull this off through blended learning, and work with maintained sector schools to create learning and resourcing partnerships to enable blended learning to happen, we may well see the end of educational apartheid in the UK and affordable quality education for all. If the two sectors are unable to work together for political, social or ideological reasons we may still see a narrowing of the gap between schools which charge fees and those which do not. The winners from disruptive technologies should always be customers. In our business that means parents, but ultimately their children. This is something to strive for!

Is it possible to make our quality more affordable? Yes, through constant refinement. It depends how you define quality. In terms of the end product achievement there is sufficient evidence to show that there are enhancements within the online product which cannot be achieved without significant investment in the face to face scenario. The online product needs developing quickly if it is to become a market leading product. This depends on organisational buy-in to what we want to achieve. It also depends on organisational courage to risk investment in a new area, and ensure there is no detraction from the core purpose and high end offering in the initial innovation period.

If a school looks to blended learning as an opportunity to cut costs, this is the wrong approach. Then the impact on our schools will be the narrowing of focus, redundancies for teachers, lower morale and a leaner, but lower quality product. If a school, on the other hand, decides to look at the ways in which blended learning can produce a better education for the child, the impact on the school, and on schooling, will be much more profound and positive. Teachers will be developed professionally, deployed with regard to their strengths, and have the opportunity to develop more individual learning relationships with their students. Children will develop technological skills, be able to work at their own pace, and develop along a pathway appropriate to them. They will be more engaged with the business of learning, and yet have the flexibility to develop their extra-curricular talents and interests. There is a broad streak of idealism in this, but there should be a healthy amount of idealism in the business of educating young people ... shouldn't there?

Schools themselves have an opportunity which needs to be grasped. But schools do not act. Leaders act. The question is whether the leaders of our schools are bold enough to take action.

# Chapter 7

# The Cloud: implications for education

**I don't need a hard disk in my computer if I can get to the server faster ... carrying around these non-connected computers is byzantine by comparison**

Steve Jobs

THE TITLE of this book is 'Classroom in the Cloud' for a number of reasons. First of all, I thought that it would conjure up a feeling of something ethereal which is not yet tangible. Second, when we talk about having our 'head in the clouds' we talk about dreaming. I could have called the book 'Head In The Clouds', but it would have implied that this was a book about a maverick Headteacher. I may be accused of this, (and certainly have been in the past!), but my focus in this book was on the impact on learning and schools, rather than a book about leadership although the final chapter focuses on the importance of leadership in the e-learning revolution. Naturally, the title also tapped in to the new phenomenon in computing which is also affecting all of us: cloud technology. I have not mentioned this so far, but it is important that I do. Schools are not only faced with innovation in education and schooling, but also face key business decisions about how they manage their IT. This impacts on the decisions which schools need to take about infrastructure, security of information, purchase of licenses, staffing of IT support and the facilitation of the whole business of the school. There is confusion about what 'the cloud' actually is, and how it may help a school. There is also a nervousness abroad concerning the security of a school's information. We need to gain some clarity about cloud computing and how it might affect our schools.

So what is the cloud? Everybody seems to have at least a vague idea, and everyone seems to be talking about it, but cloud computing is not the easiest term to define. We all use cloud based services such as Twitter, Gmail and Google and are happy to do so up to a point. But something about the proliferation of all these services and the power of the companies behind them have caused us to be rather nervous.

The importance of a cloud from a consumer viewpoint is that it enables self provisioning, so that a user can provision facilities without any human interaction; service delivery over a network; accessibility by a wide range of devices; and rapid elasticity in order that a business, or a school, can upscale or downscale computer activity. The cloud service provider, on the other hand, can distribute services as and when the customer needs them; measure usage; and as a consequence bill them accurately.

From a school's point of view, the level of security is often a concern. There is some very sensitive data held in schools about students, their families and employees. The providers of cloud services say that this is easily dealt with. Because they are operating on a much greater scale, and with a dependence on the confidence of their customers they have invested in, and learnt about, top quality security which is often far superior to that which a school might have on its own system. When one considers the scale of operation that a company like Amazon runs through a cloud service, with millions of people entrusting them with credit card and address details, why should it be harder to trust Amazon's cloud service, Amazon Web Services?

Schools then worry about where their information will be situated. In the EU there are storage rules enshrined in law about personal information, for instance, which cannot be held outside the EU. In the USA, however, the Patriot Act compels US companies to hand over data which they keep on their servers if requested to do so by the US Government. If a US company has a European server, this would still fall under the Patriot Act and so it makes users nervous.

Along with cloud services comes virtualisation. This technique involves using virtual resources instead of physical ones, so if a server is working at only 20% of its capacity, the resources which it is not currently using can be reallocated for something else. This drives up usage rates and helps a business (or a school) to reduce the number of servers. This saves on maintenance and energy costs, and many schools have gone along the virtualisation pathway. On a larger scale, this virtualisation has assisted in the development of cloud servers, as it has increased their capacity to deliver services to users.

Finally, another part of the cloud is software delivery. This helps to solve various issues such as over-provisioning, security updates and licensing.

On balance, although there are some security worries about cloud computing, the facility allows for major savings of time, energy, and maintenance while providing reassurance that a cloud server can deliver reliability which an in-house model may not provide. By the end of 2012, 20% of businesses were believed to have no IT departments, making for huge staffing cost savings. Schools have been slower to follow suit, but where business enterprises move in IT, schools often follow. With budgets, and especially staffing budgets, close to their limits it makes sense for a school looking at a blended learning option to consider the benefits of moving to a cloud server provider.

## Which type of cloud for a school?
There are a couple of different options available for schools who decide to go down the route of cloud services. On the one hand, the public cloud can be a financially appealing way forward. The school would be charged a monthly fee, depending on the volume of usage. The cloud provider then bears the whole cost of maintenance of the infrastructure. There is then no need for the school to worry about staffing its own maintenance, or investing in storage hardware which has become a growing financial burden as use and storage volumes increase. A school taking on blended learning will be likely to see storage volume rise significantly, and this needs consideration. The school will also be made free from concerns in planning capacity of use. The cloud provider charges by usage, and so there is no over-provision or under-provision which affects the school. The main disadvantage of the public cloud is security, and worries about information on students and employees being released into the public domain. This is coupled with other concerns a school may have about being made legally responsible for any such eventuality.

An alternative is a private cloud. Hardware and software is all provided by the school. This depends on virtualisation added to software which allows everyone in the school to use the cloud as a centralised resource pool. The school bears the responsibility and cost of buying hardware, software, maintenance and storage. As a result it is still expensive. But there are advantages such as speed of connection, due to the smaller, private network which is utilised, and the lack of security issues because the school keeps all of its information secure in the private cloud. This is also an automated system, which reduces the need for an IT department to constantly be on hand to fix issues. However, this removes the ability of a school to monitor who is using what, which means that it is harder to pick up on areas of wastage.

There is a third way which schools may find suits them better – and especially where access to myriad resources for blended learning through the internet is concerned. This is a hybrid cloud, incorporating some services in a private cloud, but many in a public one. The hybrid cloud can still be managed by one provider, and confidential information which is personal to students and their families can be located on the private cloud with everything else hosted publicly.

## Cloud computing concerns

- Fear of Change: As we have discussed, this is the most prevalent reason for a school not to move entirely to the cloud. This is not just about the difficulty of adapting to something new. People like upgrades, and especially if they see immediate benefits and can use the new system every day. But there are difficulties in learning new skills, plus a natural scepticism about whether new software or systems will actually make a genuine difference to the life of the member of staff.
- Human Factor: The change may come along with less palatable changes such as the threat to IT department jobs. These are colleagues that teachers value and know. Any redundancies within a school hit morale and make surviving employees nervous, so this has to be very carefully managed. In addition, there is the fact that people are the users, and the likelihood of the technology working well will depend very much on the user's capability or willingness to change.
- Reliability: there is a fear that fast, internet access may not be possible, and then how will the user manage to access their work? What is the fall-back position?
- Losing Control: A school is a place which thrives on systems working and rules being kept. This means that many of those in leadership positions in schools rely on keeping a controlled environment. But cloud computing is out-sourcing, and means a loss of control of everything from managing mistakes to keeping data secure.
- Failure of the cloud system: Clearly, a school does not want to lose its ability to function online – and especially if it has a significant amount of blended learning going on. It is important not to forget that a cloud service is likely to have a back-up called into action very quickly indeed, and issues are likely to be resolved more quickly than any in-house team can manage.
- Is it really value for money? This is a legitimate concern, as there have certainly been other technological innovations which have claimed they will be money savers, and yet have drawn businesses

in to investing more than ever in their IT budgets. There are no guarantees that fees for use of the cloud will not move upwards as businesses become more dependent on use. However, these are questions which can legitimately asked at the point of engagement. Also, schools have some genuine advantages over other businesses. Microsoft, for instance, has recently announced free storage for schoolchildren and teachers using its cloud system.

- Is it still too early? There is an element of waiting to see what the real benefits are before a school leaps into the cloud, and yet this is something we have touched on elsewhere in the book with regard to developing the IT learning capability for the school as a whole. There is an obvious sense in reticence about moving all services to the cloud before there is sufficient information available to confirm the promises that cloud service providers make, but there have been firms offering such a service for 15 years now, and in technology terms that is a long time.
- Following the crowd: Many schools worry that they might be swept up in a mad rush for the cliff edge concerning cloud computing simply because there are many people saying that this is the future. It is obviously right to remain circumspect. Just like blended learning, there is not a 'one size fits all' cloud model. A school should consider carefully how the cloud will help it achieve its strategic learning and efficiency goals before taking any rash decisions.

## Cloud computing benefits

- Cost savings: This is likened to renting a car and paying for it only when you use it, without the up-front costs such as road tax and insurance. The cloud is a "pay as you go" service.
- Security: Many argue that, despite fears to the contrary, cloud computing is more secure than a company holding its information physically, or within a private cloud. This is because cloud service providers have invested in the cloud security in a large way to protect their customers, and in doing so their own reputations.
- Flexibility: This really helps with blended learning. Teachers and students can collaborate across time zones and different locations. Students can access a school from other countries. New tools and software can easily be added to the cloud, and the most up to date software is guaranteed, which an old licensing model may not have been able to provide.
- Budgeting: A school moves from capital expenditure on hardware and software which hit budgets hard to simply renting an infrastructure and services from the cloud provider. It is an easily planned operational expense.

- Scale: A school can scale up operations, infrastructure, software and then shrink down again (for instance during holiday periods), as a school responds to peaks and troughs in user demand. No longer does a school have to pay up front for hardware and software based on predicted demand in the hope that they would meet demand and not over-compensate.
- Energy issues: Having less physical equipment such as servers, cabling and switches on a school site reduces the carbon footprint considerably and is much more energy efficient. As well as being greener, this is also a financial saving which may run to thousands per annum in a school.
- Performance: The service level agreements from cloud service providers act as guarantees of excellent performance. They promise compensation should systems go down, and maintenance is second to none as so many users are relying on them. Gone are the days of a school's own rather unreliable technician or network manager being unavailable for several hours overnight, or failing to prioritise.
- Productivity: Anywhere access to data at any time allows children and teachers to work at a time that suits them. It enables blended learning, but also means that administrative tasks can be put to bed at a convenient time. This also means that teachers, pupils and other staff can balance their time more effectively.
- Technical focus: Trusting applications, infrastructure and services to a cloud service provider means that any IT staff the school retains can have a very clearly defined role. This may lead to a reduction in the need for staffing, or a more highly tuned team. This feeds the productivity of the school.

## The future for cloud computing?

Far be it from me to try to predict the future. I am no expert in this area by any means. However, it is important that schools have some idea where cloud computing may be heading before making any major decisions. So I have looked at the predictions made by some commentators which have appeared in the press in recent times. (Source: *The Ultimate Guide To Cloud Computing*, 2012).

According to research company IDC, the cloud computing market will grow from $21.5bn to $72.9bn between 2010 and 2015. Cisco's Cloudwatch report (June 2012) found that cloud computing was on the agenda of 90% of IT decision makers, up from 52% the previous year. Of those companies who had already invested in cloud technology, 85% reported that they would be investing in it further the following year. These are big percentages! In the year from 2011 to 2012, cost reduction had jumped from the fifth most important concern to the number one spot.

There is certainly a feeling that security of data has become less of a concern and inhibitor to entry into the cloud services area for businesses since 2010. This is due to the obvious interest the cloud service providers have to maintain exceptional security levels. Another driver in the business world has been the need for firms to remain flexible and responsive to market needs.

Werner Vogels, CTO of Amazon Web Services is quoted as saying: "when it comes to cloud, we're still at day one. Enterprises will look much different in ten or twenty years."

Academics at the LSE recently delivered a research paper, commissioned by Microsoft, predicting enormous growth in industries reliant on cloud technology between 2012 and 2014. For instance the job creation in the smartphone industry was likely to be 359%, compared to aerospace, which would be around 55%. The report's authors (Liebenau, J. Karrberg, P., Grous, A., Castro, D.) wrote that cloud services would be a major driver for European growth. They recommended that policy makers in European countries should therefore follow three guidelines:

- Provide incentives for companies to adopt green energy practices (which would lead to more adoption of the cloud).
- Ensure data transfer policies do not impede growth of the cloud.
- Provide improved education and training in eSkills (which has obvious implications for the education sector and the development of online learning, sponsored by governments, in schools).

## Major changes predicted in the near future are:

- Rapid spread of the cloud to small businesses.
- Most software is being delivered via subscription.
- Big shifts to hybrid cloud as firms become much smarter about what they move to the cloud
- Further work on security systems
- More community clouds for like-minded groups (such as schools).
- More accurate measuring of IT use in firms, increasing budgeting efficiency.
- Rise in capacity for remote working in businesses (which will be translatable to online schooling). Also a change from the 9-to-5 work culture.

There are some significant implications for schools of the advent of cloud computing, and especially the sharing, collaboration and software possibilities which are offered to schools seeking to expand blended learning. In addition, the environmental and financial implications of out-sourcing to cloud services are worthy of research and consideration. The online classroom, which has begun to move towards the blended classroom, will be the 'Classroom in the Cloud' before too long. Schools have big decisions to make about how they choose to evolve and grow.

# Chapter 8

# The international dimension: opportunity or threat?

**For all the well-intentioned efforts of past governments we are still
falling further behind the best-performing school systems in the world.
In Shanghai and Singapore, South Korea and Hong Kong – indeed even in
Taiwan and Vietnam – children are learning more and performing better
with every year that passes – leaving our children behind in the global race.**

Michael Gove, Secretary of State for Education,
comments in Parliament on the PISA results, 3 December, 2013

I MADE a claim earlier in this book that UK education is the best in
the world. This seems, in some senses, to be over-playing our hand
somewhat. We are hardly topping the PISA tables, after all. We
constantly hear in the press about children in Finland, Shanghai, Korea or
the Czech Republic who could wipe the floor with us at mathematics and
science. We are behind Poland, despite the fact that in real terms Polish
teachers are paid less than half the salary of British teachers.

I have then mentioned the fact that we are further behind some
other countries in the adoption and development of blended learning.
Governments in America and the Middle East have poured money into this
area, and there are now well-developed initiatives in government schools in
these regions.

Meanwhile, private education is also adopting these models. Nord
Anglia Education – a UK and Hong Kong-owned company which runs

British schools worldwide – have increased their levels of BYOD provision across their schools in a deal with Xirrus. This fits well with their 'Global Classroom' in which children in all of their schools from China and Thailand to Hungary and Switzerland, and from the USA and Bratislava to Cambodia and Abu Dhabi communicate with one another on cross-continental learning projects.

The growth of schools offering a British education abroad to ex-patriot families, but also to home-based students is exponential. Of some concern is the fact that these schools are desperate to hire British native speakers, preferably trained in British universities, and with experience of working in UK schools. In March, 2013 a report by the *Times Educational Supplement* suggested that as many as 500,000 UK trained teachers would be required to teach overseas within the next ten years. Take a moment to consider what that might mean for UK schools. An exodus of some of our best teachers, courted by private fee-paying schools abroad, some of whom may offer lucrative tax free salaries, or at least salaries which would be subject to tax at a more preferential rate than in the UK.

The flip side is that if these overseas schools have invested in blended or online learning, they may be able to source their UK teaching talent online. Here is an opportunity for UK schools. Can we market some of our best teachers, offer their online lessons for a fee, and thereby generate an income for our schools, while retaining our talent? After all, a school in Dubai will not pay the tax-free salary, accommodation and flights home each year if they can pay a few thousand pounds for a suite of online lessons which can then be used in-house. The upshot is that the UK can keep very talented teachers, who can develop online resources, for use in our own schools, and meanwhile create an income stream which can be used for further online research and development, or the creation of the online lessons for our own students.

Which schools will be able to sell their teachers' talents in this way? Good independent schools with top-class reputations may be first in the queue, but these will also perhaps be hamstrung by the 'incumbents' dilemma'. Therefore there is an opportunity for good teachers at any other school, capable of producing high quality online lessons, to promote their schools and themselves. By offering the first eight ten-minute videos for free, the appetite of the foreign purchaser can be whetted, and thereafter a full iGCSE or A-level course could be offered for sale.

Those independent schools who do take the plunge can trade off their own names or, for ease of production, might form a consortium with other independent schools. It is not beyond the realms of possibility that a clutch of five or six schools, offering two mathematics teachers each from some of the best-known schools in the world could put together a single Mathematics iGCSE course, and even offer some online support, at a fee which might be paid by an overseas school or indeed by a family with some money, but insufficient to pay the full boarding fee which might access one of the schools full-time. This is also a fantastic opportunity for selective day schools which are at the top of the academic league tables in both the independent and state sectors, to access a hitherto closed market of overseas students who want some of the best teaching from top quality academic institutions, but never could have enrolled in the day school before.

It is certainly the case that the UK star has not yet faded overseas. Between 2009 and 2012, the numbers of independent school pupils fell by 2%, which can be put down to rising prices, or the recession. However, this downturn in numbers becomes more worrying for the independent sector when one considers that over the same period, there was an increase in numbers of overseas boarders. The increase between 2011 and 2012 alone was 5.8%. The total number of non-British as a percentage of boarders in UK schools has grown from 29.6% (2010) to 35.7% (2013) according to the Independent Schools Council (ISC) census data.

It is worrying for the independent sector because it demonstrates that it is losing market share at home. It is encouraging for British education that in the time of a worldwide economic downturn, overseas families were willing to invest heavily in a British education. We are still seen as offering a top quality product.

But before we get carried away, we need to take care. This is not the full picture. In the meantime, American, Canadian and Australian schools were also seeing major increases, and these were facilitated by very favourable visa rules at just the time when the UK government was making it harder for foreign students to access our institutions. I attended a recruitment event in Foshan, China in June 2014 and I often heard from prospective families that they were reading in the press that the UK did not want Asian students. I had to work hard to convince them that we do.

There were American institutions at this event, as there have been at many others that I have attended in recent years. It was interesting to note that the Chinese still see A levels, and increasingly the IB, as more valuable than the American qualifications. They are more interested in sending their children to America for university education. One of the reasons often stated is that America is not as safe for children as the UK. So, we have the qualifications, the fine teaching, the reassuring safety, the experience, and the quality which overseas parents want for their children. We are shooting ourselves in the foot, however, with our visa rules. Meanwhile, our English-speaking competitors are learning, and they also have some very high quality facilities, excellent teaching, scholarship programmes and other incentives (even a promise of citizenship in Canada for those who graduate from their universities).

I have travelled quite extensively to China in recent years, and something has struck me lately which is another potential cloud on the horizon. Only two or three years ago, Chinese students were coming to the UK in droves. Their language skills were variable, and they wanted our education because of the opportunities which it would give them to develop their understanding, their linguistic capability and their potential to have a career in the West. Recently, the students I have been talking to have a much better command of English. They are still keen to extricate themselves from the traditional and rather rigid Chinese high school curriculum. They are more aware of British culture and willing to engage with their British classmates. They still seek careers abroad after graduation. However, the Chinese government and education boards are facing a crisis. They have been seeing large numbers of their children and young adults leave for secondary or undergraduate education overseas. The best students stay to complete degrees and then take Masters or PhD programmes. By the time they complete their education, it is difficult for them to return home and find high quality employment in China, but there are lots of opportunities in the US, Canada, or Europe. Almost 50% of young people who leave China to be educated abroad do not return. As a result, China faces a human resources crisis. Their most talented young people are leaving.

In the autumn of 2013 there was a distinct shift in attitudes. Chinese government officials I spoke with were keen to make links with UK schools in order to promote teacher and pupil exchanges, and were also developing internship programmes in Chinese firms for students to come back to in their summer vacations. They are also setting up a great many international schools offering US, Canadian, Australian and British examination programmes alongside their Chinese curriculum. This is in an attempt to keep High School students in China for longer by offering greater breadth of curriculum choice, and stem the brain drain as much as possible. Incentives are being offered for Chinese graduates to return home.

I have visited several of these international schools. In Beijing High School No. 80 I was impressed by the group work, small classes, facilities, excellent level of English instruction and numbers of ex-pat European students whose parents were choosing a Chinese government school for their continuing education. At Dalian University of Technology affiliated High School I was shown around an extraordinary new build campus, spoke with the Principal about his vision of developing his students' world view, and discussed the pupil and teacher exchanges which were ongoing with several countries. At Peking University Institute of Education I discussed with Professor Zhang Yajie and Associate Dean Bao Xuechao their plans to develop a centre to support families of children who were studying within the international schools in order that they can involve families in the educational process and help them to understand a Western system of tutorial support and learning. China has a need for our teaching methods, and a healthy respect for what we produce. However, it is also rightly proud of its own educational tradition based on academic rigour and Confucianism. It does not want its children to lose this, and does not want to lose its children.

In fact, I liked what I was seeing in China, but the reason that I was disturbed is that, when one considers the reliance on Chinese students which our schools have currently, the last thing we want to do is lose the Chinese to a cheaper, growing, and, possibly in the future, better system on offer to them at home. ISC figures show that in 2013 51% of boarders at GSA schools, 36.2% of boarders at HMC schools, and 37.5% of boarders at IAPS schools came from China and Hong Kong. These three groups of independent schools alone were educating Chinese students who accounted for 48.9% of all overseas boarding pupils in UK schools. China is a massive and lucrative market for us, and we cannot afford to lose it. However, while we are still flavour of the month in China, and have a product they like, we need to perhaps rethink the way in which we engage with the Chinese market. We need to consider what we can offer them in order to maintain our credibility and mark of quality while continuing to have a lucrative relationship with them. Blended and online learning may well be an answer for us.

I mention China because of the recent experience I have had in the region. I have also been aware in recent years of the precarious nature of other overseas markets for British schools, and the need to constantly stay on top of changes. I have twice travelled to Thailand, and will do again this year. Thai students are excellent, but Bangkok is full of British, American and Australian schools, and the economic fluctuations in value of the pound versus the Australian dollar can make the market fluctuate in our favour, or against us. Russia is a huge market for the UK, and A levels are again seen as a strong curriculum offering. However, recent political events and economic sanctions against Russia by the West may work against us. Just before the Ukraine conflict, Putin announced a billion pound 'student grant' to encourage students to study abroad. The future of this incentive may well hang in the balance. Can British schools rely on Russian boarders for much longer? If not, can we engage in a market which we know likes what we offer, but for whom we may soon be out of reach? If so, we will again have to think creatively.

The Middle East is a third area of interest, threat or opportunity. It is another region where the growth in British curriculum schools has been encouraging. There is certainly plenty of money available to Arab families should they wish to send children to UK schools. However, there are cultural reasons for keeping children at home, and the ability of those setting up schools to offer tax-free incentives to UK teachers. I have mentioned earlier the initiative to develop BYOD across schools in the region, sponsored by government with iPads in every classroom. The UAE is developing its own expertise in online learning which eclipses ours, and so we will have to engage intelligently in this market.

We need to be alive to the possibilities, but also wary of the changes which are affecting our currently lucrative markets. There are possibilities in South America, India and Africa. There is also something to be said for entering a market which is developing, but with a new offer. If North American families are embracing online learning, why not offer them a British alternative? The only thing limiting us is our willingness or ability to develop and grow in exciting ways. We need to develop an entrepreneurial spirit among our school leaders, and thereby gain a competitive advantage. The children in our schools will benefit by all that we can learn and develop through such engagement with the worldwide market.

# Chapter 9

# Conclusion: the importance of independent leadership

We are all prisoners of our past. It is hard to think of things except in the way we have always thought of them. But that solves no problems and seldom changes anything.

Charles Handy, The Age of Unreason, 1990

C HILDREN LIVE in the present. They do not have much of a past. Yet they attend schools which are in many ways run in a similar vein to those which their parents, grandparents and great grandparents attended. The welfare state was largely responsible for extending that provision which the industrial revolution had begun the century before. But the nature of schools has changed very little until the end of the 20th century. If leaders run them without thinking of things in a new way, we will run the risk of imprisoning a new generation. We must act!

The millennium was an important time for education. The coming of a new century was an opportunity for horizon scanning, and academics looked to the 21st Century with interest and enthusiasm. They all believed passionately that it was time we re-thought education. There was even a name for it: 'De-schooling'.

In 2001, the OECD 'Schooling For Tomorrow' project developed six scenarios which described options for schooling in 2020. They represented a range of positioning, from the *status quo* through to re-schooling and de-schooling (examined in Mulford, 2008).

Scenario 1, 'Bureaucracy', looked at the status quo, and the type of schooling which would persist if school leaders did not countenance change. What was envisaged was strong pressure for accountability, and the development of strong administrative capacities to handle the increasing bureaucratic demands this would entail. Leadership would involve juggling competing vested interests in a scenario of limited extra resources but the continual addition of new expectations and demands. This scenario was unattractive and unsustainable. There are echoes of it in more traditional schools today in which teachers and leaders chase their tails following initiatives and parental demands. It is a burn-out scenario. It is horrible.

Scenarios 2 and 3, 'Social Centres' and 'Learning organisations' were more appealing. In one type of scenario, there was an increased emphasis on the social agenda. Such schools acted as scaffolding for communities and families in the face of social fragmentation. There are some parts of the UK which undoubtedly have seen the development of this type of scenario in their schools, which now double as community centre, religious centre, citizens advice bureau and clinic – if not in actual fact, certainly in the demands being placed upon school staff. Meanwhile the 'Learning Organisation' focused on a high quality learning agenda, developing learning opportunities for experimentation, innovation and extension of collaborative opportunities. This is the attractive face of re-schooling which has provided the ground for blended learning to flourish, and I would suggest bridges over to Scenario 4, 'ICT Networks', in the de-schooling category.

In this scenario, dissatisfaction with institutional provision, and diversified demand, leads to an abandonment of schools as formal structures in favour of a multitude of learning networks provisioned by powerful, inexpensive ICT: 'The deinstitutionalising, even dismantling, of school systems is part of the emerging 'network society'.

It links with Scenario 5, 'Market', in which the market for education provision is significantly extended as diversification is encouraged and many new providers with diverse educational offerings enter the market place.

These latter three scenarios combine to produce what we have been describing. It was envisaged as early as 2001. It was assumed that such trends would have emerged by 2020. We are six years away as I write, and the OECD study appears remarkably prophetic. (Scenario 6, 'Meltdown', envisaged huge teacher shortages and an ageing teacher profession with low morale leading to an exodus from teaching. This has not occurred, but without significant changes it may).

By 2008, Ben Harris and Nolan Estes were able to identify nine goals for change for the American school system. Based in Austin, these academics from the University of Texas outlined an inspiring vision for future education, stating that the school of the future must be one that is fundamentally different from the one that we have had for about 100 years:

> Programme assessment will shift from gazing in the rear view mirror to focusing on progress towards goals ... The fundamentally different school that we envision is one that makes the growth and developments of mature adults its primary mission ... If the school of the future can bring students, schooling, family and community together in meaningful, satisfying ways it can serve both individual learning needs and those of the larger society.

In all scenarios, challenges are presented for school leaders. In all scenarios, change was seen as likely, or even unavoidable. Leaders need to manage change, and sponsor those agents of change within their schools who can deliver the kinds of outcomes which we would like to see. Being prisoners of our past is not an option. Julie Lindsay, the founder of Flat Classroom, about whom I wrote earlier in this book, introduces the concept of the 'teacherpreneur' who sees the opportunity for collaborative, connected learning and as a result creates the opportunities for the flat classroom. But she is also very clear about the importance of leadership in schools in order that such creativity and energy does not wither on the vine:

> There must be support within the school for teachers who want to take risks and try new techniques and ideas. Otherwise serious and lasting change cannot be sustained.

Chris Day, Ken Leithwood *et al* were commissioned by the National College for Leadership of Schools and Children's Services to investigate the impact of Headteachers, producing *10 Strong Claims About Successful School Leadership* (2010). Their findings are very significant for any change proposed in schools, and demonstrate clearly that the classroom teacher, while hugely influential in the lives of the children they come into contact with on a daily basis, can only be as effective as the school's leadership will allow. The 10 strong claims include:

1. Headteachers are the main source of leadership in their schools.
2. There are eight key dimensions of successful leadership.
3. Headteachers' values are key components in their success.
4. Successful heads use the same basic leadership practices, but there is no single model for achieving success.
5. Differences in context affect the nature, direction and pace of leadership actions.
6. There are three broad phases of leadership success.
7. Heads contribute to student learning and achievement through a combination and accumulation of strategies and actions.

8. Heads grow and secure success by layering leadership strategies and actions.
9. Successful Heads distribute leadership progressively.
10. The successful distribution of leadership depends on the establishment of trust.

The study was one of the biggest of its kind ever funded worldwide, and the biggest ever undertaken in the UK. It considered the impact of leadership on pupil outcomes, and investigated a national sample of schools which had improved results under the same Headteacher over a three-year period. The research found that successful leaders define these outcomes not only in terms of test and examination results, but also in terms of social outcomes, pupil and staff motivation, engagement and well-being, the quality of teaching and learning, and the school's contribution to the community. It found that successful heads improve these outcomes through who they are – their values, virtues, attributes, dispositions and competencies – as well as the strategies they enact and the ways in which they adapt their leadership skills to their context. The upshot is, Headteachers are vitally important in implementing the changes which improve outcomes for children in our schools.

If we are not careful, we can regard technology in schools as being about "stuff" and "things". We talk about technology in schools in terms of money and budgets. We tear out our hair over the need for training and provision. We feel that we are being left behind, and do not have sufficient hours in the day to reach the level of personal competence and skill to make appropriate decisions, relying on those within the school who we hope have the competence. But Headteachers need to be absolutely in tune with what is possible, and how it impacts on the core business of our schools: teaching and learning. We need to take care of our children and their teachers, who are our employees. We need to train both students and their teachers in order that they can be confident and happy, and we need to distribute leadership effectively and fairly in order that the school community as a whole can understand the path that we have chosen to take. As with any other major decision facing a school, we should be guided by what is in the best interests of the children. This is hard, because we may just be at the point at which UK education needs to set sail into an uncertain future. Our school leaders need to be brave, adaptable and willing to learn as they go. These qualities will inspire confidence and followership in their staff, in the parents who entrust them with the care of their children, and with governors and politicians who require reassurance in order that they can step back from day-to-day management and allow the Head to lead.

Our Heads are at the very centre of the learning revolution which is taking place in our schools, and they have an enormous responsibility, not only to the children and teachers in their own schools, but to the children and teachers in our nation.

Top down initiatives from government will not be espoused by teachers. Teacher enthusiasts will not be able to create a revolution on their own – at least not one which has the capacity to last. Headteachers must engage with this, make a decision on their own school's strategy for e-learning, and implement a plan to take this forward. If they fail to take the initiative now, our education system will cease to be one of the pre-eminent secondary education systems in the world. This is important, because our current world status brings us an influx of overseas students, investment and exposure to the outside world. It prevents us from becoming an isolated rock in the sea.

Heads are important for one fundamental reason: they keep the business of educational change focused on the business of teaching and learning. Business managers and bursars look at staff salary costs, IT infrastructure costs, and maintenance issues. All these are vitally important to get right, but need to be addressed in the overall desire to provide the highest quality education rather than the most efficient model. Education is worth paying for if it is a quality offering. Although I have spent much of this book advocating that schools dive in to blended learning, and act more from impulse than circumspection, I am not in favour of this as a penny-pinching, cost-cutting exercise. It is because I believe that in the context of my own school, blended learning is the best way forward. Other heads must act within their own contexts. All of us are at different stages of development and understanding. We all have differing priorities, pressures and goals. Heads have a job to motivate teachers and pupils.

> Take any hundred books on change, and they all boil down to one word: motivation. (Fullan, 2006)

Good leadership needs to be situationally appropriate (Christensen, 2000). It needs to be resonant (Boyatzis and McKee, 2005). These latter two advocate that leaders reflect and act in the moment: exactly the type of leadership required when navigating the almost unchartered waters of blended learning:

> it is like watching a dance – there are rhythms, moves, tempos, times of leading, following, freestyle, and choreography. Mindful observance of the dance gives you important information. It reminds us to pay attention to more than the conversation, but also to the movement, mirroring, tone, intensity, and cadences … and it reminds us to pay attention to the process within us; what feelings and thoughts are evoked in us as we observe this dance?" (Boyatzis and McKee, 2005).

Actually, it is not change which is the most difficult thing ahead of us as leaders. It is the ability to take a step outside and watch the dance that is going on around us, and to be honest about the fact that some of it feels uncomfortable and needs to change. In this book I have tried to explain something which I see as an opportunity to address this change, but it is so very hard for leaders to pull off because it challenges so much about the organisations which we have grown up with, developed our career within, and now lead forward. But what is very important, as a leader, is that there are times when the well-worn path is not the path to take. This is where leadership is really required, and I believe that we are at this point in UK education now.

As leaders we have responsibilities to children, their parents, our school communities, our country, and most importantly of all, to learning. That creative impulse of curiosity which we have all felt and, perhaps, was the reason that we became teachers in the first place. If we love learning we need to nurture it, because for all the excitement that surrounds the sparkling toys of the learning revolution, there is much uncertainty and danger as well. Revolutions are notoriously bloody affairs which begin with ideas, develop with the excitement of a brave new world, and often disappoint their makers. Headteachers are in a unique position to make a difference, and to nurture learning. We are in a privileged position from which we can not only observe the dance, but also call the tune.

Leadership is hard, and calls for sacrifice. Leadership of schools especially can be isolating. Leaders carry scars from battles. It is how they learn. Taking on a disruptive technology is difficult. To embrace it, battles will need to be fought. Will our UK education leaders have the stomach for the fight? Resonant leaders, capable of acting in the moment, and learning as they navigate, do so by being authentic to their values as educators. Living these values allows them to take their schools with them. Staff, students and parents are inspired by passionate advocates of learning. School leaders who believe in learning, and can demonstrate how their school can thrive by adoption of the new learning opportunities which the disruptive technology of the internet has brought to the door, can also show a school how to embrace change. The only thing stopping us, often, is our own fear that we will make a mistake. School leaders need to demonstrate independence in the face of such change, and know their own minds. They must make the decision, and stand by it, to either embrace the disruption or weather the storm. Those who believe that their school can do something special and innovative, for the good of children and teachers, need only to make a start.

I am immensely fortunate to work at a school with a close attachment to Ely Cathedral. Several times a week I find myself at a service in one of the most awe-inspiring buildings in the United Kingdom, if not the world. Children from my school between the ages of two and 18 pass through its doors throughout their school career. Former pupils always want to visit it. The cathedral becomes part of them, whether or not they become people of faith. The experience of living and learning in this extraordinary and beautiful environment develops a spirituality and perspective which helps form the young adult who leaves the school.

All schools nurture something special in children. They plant memories in children, and these memories shape the people they become. Memories root a child within the school, and of course we hope that the memories are wholesome and nourishing. We do not always manage to get that right as educators, but our purpose is to give young people a grounding: academically, spiritually, or morally. No matter what changes beset our schools, this will remain our purpose. We develop the adults of the future. When things do go wrong, as they are bound to from time to time, our teachers and schools seek to rebuild confidence, character, understanding, commitment, pride, or whatever needs to be restored.

Schools educate such a variety of different children, and the job of teachers is as never-ending as that of a gardener. A moment's neglect has consequences. There will be elements which seek to frustrate us. Teachers and school leaders need relentless focus.

We need grounding in our principles of delivering a fine quality education, and in fact we have never lost sight of that. However, the structures of man sometimes collapse. It is the natural curiosity of pupils which keeps seeking the sun, and driving upwards. It is embedded deep within all of us, and school leaders need to create the conditions in which growth will happen, and the plant will thrive. Where schools are concerned, leaders have an enormous responsibility and an enormous opportunity. At times of disruption, however, leaders also have to be incredibly brave, and seek to take their people with them on an extraordinary, seemingly perilous journey.

Leaders who cultivate the trust of their staff and school community will be successful. They will be able to pursue their goals, directed by the compass which points to ensuring the best for the children in their school ... and there is no 'one size fits all' package. That is a ludicrous idea. There are so many schools for so many contexts. What the leader needs to do is acquire a resonance in his leadership, understand the context of his school and the people within his community, and, as with every leader, turn to face the dangers and opportunities, acting in the moment to produce what is best.

The current disruption is not a cause for wailing and gnashing of teeth. Our schools are excellent. They are staffed with highly trained, committed and intelligent people who care deeply about education. We are not all doomed.

Neither, however, is there a calm sea before us. It is turbulent and treacherous. Times of disruption call for clear leadership, clear direction, reassuring messages, planning and strategy. Occasionally the direction may seem to be turning one's back on all that one knows and holds dear, but it is the right thing to do. Those in positions of leadership must think the unthinkable, make brave decisions, and stand by them in order to endure in an uncertain future. To dare to do so in the face of the perceived wisdom of the age allows a new Gallileo to make a beneficial impact on mankind. If we sit tight, put our fingers in our ears, fail to acknowledge that the world has changed, and duck the issue, we risk making children the prisoners of our past.

I am not prepared to do that. Are you?

LIBRARY, UNIVERSITY OF CHESTER

# Further Reading

Adonis, A. (2012) *Education, Education, Education: reforming England's Schools.* London: Biteback.

Barber, M. (2000) The Evidence of Things Not Seen: Reconceptualising Public Education. Paper presented to the OECD, Schooling For Tomorrow Conference.

Boyatzis, R. and McKee, A. (2005) *Resonant Leadership Boston.* Boston: Harvard Business School Press.

Burke, L. (ed) (2014) *Learning In A Digitalized Age: Plugged in, turned on, totally engaged?* Woodbridge: John Catt Educational.

Christensen, C. (2000, 2nd Edn) *The Innovator's Dilemma: When new technologies cause great firms to fail.* Boston: Harvard Business Review Press.

Collins, J. (2001) *Good To Great.* London: Random House.

Fullan, M. (2005) *Leadership and Sustainability: system thinkers in action.* Thousand Oaks: Sage.

Fullan, M. (2006) Chapter 3 'Change' in *Turnaround Leadership* (pp. 35-68) San Francisco. Jossey-Bass.

Hargreaves, A. (2004) Inclusive and exclusive educational change: emotional responses of teachers and implications for leadership. *School Leadership & Management 24*, (2) 287-308.

Hargreaves, A. and Fink, D. (2006) *Sustainable leadership.* San Francisco: Jossey-Bass.

Harris, A. (2008) *Distributed School Leadership: Developing tomorrow's leaders.* Abingdon: Routledge.

Harris, B. and Estes, N. (2008) Visions for future schooling: an essay on promising possibilities, *International Journal of Leadership in Education,* 11(1). 103-107.

Isaacson, W. (2012) *Steve Jobs.* New York: Simon & Schuster.

Leithwood, K, Day, C., Sammons, P., Harris, A. and Hopkins, D. (2010) *Ten Strong Claims about Successful School Leadership*. Nottingham: National College for School Leadership.

Lepani, B (1994) *The New Learning Society: the Challenge for Schools*. University of Sydney: Australia.

Lucas, H. C. (2012) *The Search For Survival: Lessons from disruptive technologies*. Santa Barbara: Praeger.

McGrath, A. (2013) *Lifting our Heads*. Woodbridge: John Catt Educational.

Mulford, B. (2008) Organisation: Schools of the Future Section 3. The Leadership Challenge: Improving Learning In Schools. *Australian Education Review*, 53. Camberwell, Australia.

Pfeffer, J. (2007) *What Were They Thinking?: Unconventional wisdom about management*. Boston: Harvard Business School Press.

Robinson, K (2001) *Out Of Our Minds: Learning to be creative*. Chichester: Capstone.

Robinson, K. with Aronica, L. (2009) *The Element: How finding your passion changes everything*. London, Penguin.

# Acknowledgements

This book has emerged through various circumstances, and thanks to the interventions of a number of important people.

While it is on the surface a book about technology, it is first and foremost a book about learning, leadership and daring to think outside the box. In developing my own capacity for all these, I have a whole host of people to whom I should be grateful.

My wife, Claire is one of the finest teachers I know, and has taught me about creativity, commitment and how to push the boundaries. Her support strengthens me in all aspects of my life. My parents believed in learning, and sent me to a school which challenged me. They, and my teachers, taught me to think differently. I owe an enormous debt to those who taught me about leadership at Nottingham University School of Education – particularly Chris Day, Qing Gu and Belinda Harris. Their teaching was the most challenging that I have ever experienced and opened the educational landscape before me, encouraging criticality and the capacity for re-imagining education.

In my work I have been fortunate to come across many fine colleagues whose professionalism and creativity benefit the children they teach immeasurably. It is these teachers whom I think of when placing the primacy of the relationship between pupil and teacher at the heart of considerations of efficient and innovative models for schools. Liam Webster, Marc Hawes, Jane Thomas, Ned Kittoe, John Morley, James Postle, Charles Conway, Alan Scadding, Nigel Reynolds, Bill Hardiman, John Shoard, Jonathan Coller, John Cantrell, Rodger Alderson, Ian Leverton, Richard Simpson, Nick Born and Chris Reid have all played a part in the development of the ideas contained within this book.

I owe a debt to Charles Paumelle for introducing me to the world of Coursera, Daphne Koller for her encouragement, Sir Ken Robinson for his inspiration, and Nick Donoghue for always helping me to see the simplicity of the technology through the jargon. In addition, Alex Sharratt and Jonathan Barnes at John Catt Educational have encouraged and helped focus my ideas, to say nothing about providing the polish necessary to produce a finished product.

My perspective on world education has been shaped by my experience of hundreds of children in the schools in which I have taught, but also many that I have visited overseas. I thank Jamie Jin at CIE (formerly the British Council), Wu Xinping, Yajie Zhang of PKU College Beijing, Mark Logan of Nord Anglia, Shireen Lawrence (formerly of GEMS), Julia Verkade, Colwyn Williams, Barbara and Theresa Glasmacher, Pippa Watts, Noa Guo, Yuan Ya, and David Mansfield.

Eddie Falshaw, Mungo Dunnett, Ian Yorston and Gerry Holden were all good enough to read the initial manuscript, point out flaws, suggest improvements, and encourage my efforts. I am fortunate to have the support of my Chair of Governors, Jeff Hayes, and Principal Sue Freestone who encourage me in my endeavours and offer constant support.

My children Rosie, Billy and Eva have put up with yet another summer holiday in which I have ensconced myself in the study. Their inspiration is a source of enormous strength and happiness. I look forward to their futures with excitement and hope.